CONSTRUCTIVE
WALLOWING

Praise for *Constructive Wallowing*

"Where cognitive therapy teaches you what's wrong with your thinking, Tina Gilbertson's *Constructive Wallowing* teaches you what's right with your feeling. Her style is light and breezy but her message is profound. Both wise and engaging—like a great therapist—this book can start you on the path of self-awareness and self-acceptance that is the essence of healing. And it's good for therapists too. I found especially useful Tina's focus on recognizing the disparaging, dismissive inner critic that keeps us stuck in our painful feelings by preventing us from really feeling and learning from them."

—Elio Frattaroli, M.D.,
author of *Healing the Soul in the Age of the Brain*

"If you've already discovered that 'Trying to think positive' only makes you feel worse, it's time to embrace *Constructive Wallowing* instead. This wise and witty book shows why pushing bad feelings away never works, and offers a practical approach to the more liberating alternative of allowing yourself to feel them. Ignore those grinning gurus: Tina Gilbertson explains how anxiety, anger, sadness, and fear can be a doorway to a far more profound kind of happiness."

—Oliver Burkeman,
author of *The Antidote: Happiness for People Who Can't Stand Positive Thinking*

"Tina has written a wise and wonderful book. Her warmth and light touch make it a pleasure to read. It's even better than that, though; were you to actually follow her advice, you would be stepping through a process that therapists and research psychologists know increases self-compassion and behavioral flexibility. Tina skillfully dismantles the all-too-common protest that being kind to yourself somehow precludes being a caring and responsible human being. She goes on to present an accessible introduction to a set of practices that can lead to good stuff for you and for the people around you (well, assuming you agree that less rigidity and wasted energy equals good). This is a book I will share with clients. I'll recommend *Constructive Wallowing* to psychology students, too, as a book that presents important research findings in a palatable-to-laypersons way."

—Roberta K. Deppe, M.A.
(counseling psychology), Ph.D. (social psychology),
adjunct instructor at Lewis & Clark College

"We've all read about different ways to stay positive and grateful, but Tina Gilbertson turns conventional wisdom on its head by suggesting that maybe we don't need to be either of those things all the time. Her helpful approach comes at a time when we could all use a healthy dollop of compassion and humor, as well as a more effective strategy for coping with difficult feelings."

—Jason Baker,
publisher of *Natural Awakenings* magazine

"When Tina talks about feelings, you want to listen, because an 'Aha' moment is usually sure to follow."

—Lisa Voisin, author of *The Watcher*

"Gilbertson's conversational tone, plain language, and step-by-step approach explain a deceptively simple concept. Recommended for a wide audience, including newbies to the self-help field and veterans of the genre."

—Alison Campbell,
acquisitions librarian at North Vancouver District
Public Library

"Tina is a gifted therapist, and has a wonderful way of talking about emotions in a manner that's accessible to everyone. She offers a fresh viewpoint on how to be with our emotions in a helpful way, embracing and accepting ourselves as we are while learning to move forward. This is a great book for anyone wanting to grow out of old patterns and move forward in an emotionally intelligent way."

—Janet Sandell, M.A., licensed professional counselor

"If I find myself ruminating over a particular problem, I now recognize that as my cue to wallow. Tina Gilbertson's *Constructive Wallowing* gave me the permission I had unknowingly craved to truly feel my feelings, heal the wounds of both my past and present, and get on with fully living my life."

—Jody Wynnyk, professional dating coach

"*Constructive Wallowing* is a revelation. Learning how to distinguish emotions from thoughts, and for the first time really believing that my emotions DO matter (and that I'm not a bad person for having them), has made my relationships with myself, my family, and my friends richer and more stable. Tina is a master at providing thorough explanations without overwhelming the reader with information. A must-read for anyone with a heart and a brain!"

—Isabel A. Spradlin, L.M.T.,
yoga instructor and massage therapist

"Tina Gilbertson is the kind of therapist to whom you would confidently send your friends and relatives. She is smart, funny, compassionate, wise, self-aware, and doesn't take herself too seriously. And did I mention that all of those qualities come through in her writing?"

—Steve Berman,
adjunct professor at Lewis & Clark College

CONSTRUCTIVE WALLOWING

HOW TO BEAT BAD FEELINGS BY LETTING YOURSELF HAVE THEM

TINA GILBERTSON

EDITIONS

Published in the United States by Viva Editions, an imprint of Cleis Press, Inc., 2246 Sixth Street, Berkeley, California 94710.

Printed in the United States.
Cover design: Scott Idleman/Blink
Cover illustration: iStockphoto
Text design: Frank Wiedemann

First Edition.
10 9 8 7 6 5 4 3 2 1

Trade paper ISBN: 978-1-936740-80-2
E-book ISBN: 978-1-936740-96-3

Library of Congress Cataloging-in-Publication Data

Gilbertson, Tina.
 Constructive wallowing / by Tina Gilbertson.
    pages cm
 ISBN 978-1-936740-80-2 (alk. paper)
 1. Emotions. 2. Self-help techniques. I. Title.
 BF561.G55 2013
 152.4--dc23
                        2013025746

CONTENTS

THE WONDERFUL WORLD OF WALLOWING

I like the phrase "constructive wallowing" because the pieces seem to contradict each other. *Constructive* is a good thing, but *wallowing* is bad. Right?

If this odd combination of words caught your attention, maybe it's because you think wallowing in feelings, especially rotten ones, is just not a great use of your time. I can understand that; most people would rather spend their down time alphabetizing their cleaning supplies than stewing about office politics or crying over things they can't control.

But if you're not taking the time to pay attention to all your emotions, including the so-called "negative" ones, you could be seriously missing out. I mean on *life*. You could be passing up the good stuff: happiness, growth, and emotional freedom. You could be saying, "No thanks!" to more motivation, interest, and energy to pursue your dreams.

Emotions *are* energy. All of them—not just the good ones. Would you willingly shut off your own power source?

As a mental health counselor working with individual adults, I often hear people who are unhappy about something say, "I don't want to *wallow*." They usually say the word as if they're talking about licking the bottom of a wading pool in a doggie daycare facility.

And while I understand perfectly that wallowing in yucky feelings is unpleasant, I still like to answer, "Why not? What's so bad about wallowing?" (I can be like that, just to warn you.)

That conversation is often the beginning of a paradigm shift for the person in the client's chair. It changes their sense of the way things are, and opens up new possibilities for who they can become.

It's a shift I've been through myself, and for me it opened doors I didn't even know were there. Once I was able to understand that all my emotions were acceptable, not just the happy ones, I was able to embrace all that I am as a person. This led to a much-desired career change for me. All my life I'd known there was something special I wanted to do, if only I could figure out what it was. Learning how to deal with my feelings in a self-compassionate way helped me get in touch with my whole self, which included my purpose. It was only then that I could see the path under my feet.

I became a therapist to support others in developing compassion for themselves and all their feelings, so they could become who they're meant to be. I wanted to teach people how to wallow *constructively* so they could not only reach for their potential, but heal from past hurts and feel better about themselves right this minute.

I thought of the book's title one day after talking with a client—let's call him Vance—a financial analyst who was going through a painful breakup. I'd had scores of conversations with people in various challenging circumstances, and I was hearing for the umpteenth time from Vance the familiar "I don't want to wallow" speech.

He assured me that he didn't have the time or the desire to wallow in his feelings about losing his girl-friend. He just needed "some tools for coping better" because, as it happened, he was starting a demanding new job at the very same time.

When I asked him about it, Vance couldn't point to any ways in which he was coping badly. He was getting dressed every day, taking care of necessary tasks, even going out with friends. Suicide never entered his mind. Nevertheless, understandably, he was suffering. He was distracted by insistent feelings of sadness and anger and grief.

I remember thinking, "Why does Vance think he's not coping well, just because he's having feelings?"

The timing of the split certainly wasn't ideal; Vance could have used some down time to regroup before diving into a new job. No one wants to be sad, angry, or preoccupied while trying to learn the ropes in an unfamiliar environment. But circumstances being what they were, he just ended up with too much on his plate at once. Any human being in his position would have found it impossible to feel serene and in control the way Vance wanted to.

Like so many people I've talked with, Vance hadn't taken the time to acknowledge the intense and chal-lenging nature of his present circumstances. Without consciously deciding to, he was treating himself as a sort of superhero who could withstand a hail of emotional bullets without pausing in his forward movement, let alone being pierced. He believed he was supposed to roll with whatever came his way without missing a step or even feeling uncomfortable. He seemed to see himself as an armored robot, programmed for productivity. So when he had normal emotions that affected his mood, he thought something was wrong with him!

As I said, Vance is far from alone in thinking this way; I see this superhero mentality in one client after another who comes in stressed out, depressed, and feeling stuck.

If only everyone knew how much more *constructive* it is to *wallow* in feelings rather than trying to ignore them and forge ahead, we'd all be able to move forward in work and in love without getting stuck so often in what feels like emotional quicksand.

The breakup-and-new-job combination made for a bumpy ride over the next few weeks, but Vance endured and eventually found peace, both at work and in another relationship. There's wisdom in the notion that what doesn't kill us makes us stronger. What we might need, though, is a new definition of strength that doesn't require ignoring ourselves.

If you're tired of
- **trying to ignore** difficult feelings
- **doing something constructive** every minute of the day, and/or
- **feeling down on yourself** because of a lack of motivation,

this book will offer you a practical and effective alternative to kicking yourself when you're down.

Whatever skills, habits, or tools you've already got going for you, you can keep. I'll ask you to give up only what's weighing you down and working against you. You can't lose; you can only gain.

If you'd simply like to be able to do a little wallowing and actually feel *good* about it, well, then you've come to the right place.

What Would You Do If You Lost Everything?

Natasha

Eighteen-year-old Natasha is a bright, athletic college student who loves to hike and explore the wilderness. Ever since she could walk she's spent almost all her free time in the forest on the rolling hills near her home. As a child she would often disappear among the leaves for hours, climbing trees, examining every surface, and eating the lunch she'd brought in her backpack to save her having to go home too soon.

Her parents learned not to worry because of how well she knew the forest and how agile and strong she was. Besides, it was impossible to keep her out of the woods!

Her family and friends always knew that Natasha would find a way to make a living enjoying and protecting her favorite habitat. No one was surprised when she applied and was accepted to the forestry program at the local university.

Natasha chose to continue living at home while going to school. Her parents bought her a good road bike that she could use for commuting.

One cold November morning during her very first year, as she's riding her still-new bike to the university under a threatening gray sky, a speeding car runs a red light and drives straight into Natasha. She's thrown from her bike alive but unconscious and seriously injured.

She spends the next month in a coma. When she wakes up, her mind is intact—she was wearing a helmet and escaped a brain injury—but she feels nothing below her waist.

Natasha learns that she was hit by a drunk driver at 7:45 a.m. on a Tuesday, that her spinal cord was severed irreparably, and that she's permanently lost the use of her legs.

At first she can't believe she'll never again go on long, solitary hikes off the beaten path on those forested hills, or ride the bike her parents bought her, which was mangled beyond repair. But eventually she realizes it's true; in one horrible moment, life as she knew it is over for Natasha.

In the face of this unfathomable loss, Natasha tries to maintain a positive attitude, concentrating on the fact that she survived. Her family and friends encourage her to focus on what she *can* do, not what she can't. Natasha makes everyone proud with her unconquerable spirit and will to go on.

Between rehabilitation sessions with physical and occupational therapists, she distracts herself from bad feelings about what happened with inspiring movies and healing affirmations. Whenever she starts to feel angry or blue, she turns her mind to all the things she's grateful for.

One year after the accident, Natasha's fractured bones have healed, and she's returned to college. She's become skilled at using a wheelchair to get around, but, despite her efforts to stay positive, she seems to be getting more depressed instead of less so.

Her "negative" feelings frustrate her, and she reads one inspirational book after another to keep her spirits up. One day when she's feeling especially down, she angrily thinks, "When will I move on from this?"

Dan

Twenty-eight years old and unable to find a job, Dan decides to enlist in the military. He's healthy and intelligent, but hasn't yet found his calling. He likes the thought of learning on the job and having steady employment in precarious economic times.

Maybe he'll be an Army man, he thinks, just like his uncle. But Dan is thorough. He visits recruiters from all the branches of the military before he makes his choice: The Army it will be!

In a very short time he's passed the military aptitude test with flying colors. Next he survives basic training, and, a few months after that, he's a newly minted topographic surveyor. Less than a year after enlisting, he finds himself stationed overseas.

While working with a team in the baking sun to erect a survey tower in a dusty valley, Dan notices unusual disturbances in the dirt near where they've set up. Just as he's bending down to get a better look, someone in front of him steps on a mine!

The blinding flash of light is the last thing Dan will

ever see. Projectiles from the explosion destroy both his eyes and part of his left hand, ending his short military career as well as the life he knows as a sighted person. The man who stepped on the mine is thrown several feet and badly injured, but survives. No one else is seriously hurt.

Back at home, Dan is overwhelmed by anger. "Why me?" he thinks, and punches his pillow. He wishes he'd tried harder to find a job as a civilian before joining the Army. Things would be so different if he just hadn't enlisted. What on earth was he thinking? He's plagued by regret.

He doesn't want to go through the rest of his life as a "damned cripple," and there are days when he refuses to get out of bed. Everything seems to make him angry.

Gradually Dan becomes aware of a profound sadness under the rage. He'll never see the faces of his future children, if he even has them. Thinking about what might have been, he cries wrenching tears that come from deep within his soul.

Over time, the tears fall less often. A new interest in life begins to sneak in at the edges of his grief. During his rehabilitation Dan has become adept at touch typing—so much so that he's filled several reams of paper with his thoughts, feelings, and observations. He discovers a quiet joy in writing that he's always known but never paid much attention to.

A year after the explosion, Dan has made long strides in adjusting to his disability and is filled with purpose as he works on writing his first book. He's engaged to the warm-hearted occupational therapist who patiently helped him re-train in the tasks of daily living, and they're looking forward to starting a life and a family together.

At times he's frustrated by his disability, but Dan is far from depressed. He has "up" days and "down" days, exactly like anyone else.

Why is Dan, who started out with so much regret, anger, and sadness about what happened to him, now feeling so much better than Natasha?

By the time you finish reading this book, I hope the answer will be clear.

What If You Have Everything and Still Aren't Happy?

It's easy to feel compassion for people like Natasha and Dan, whose losses are so readily apparent. But when it comes to the small losses, irritations, upsets, and annoyances that the vast majority of us suffer daily and weekly, year in and year out, how much compassion do we have for ourselves? Chances are we compare ourselves to people like Natasha and Dan and say, "It could be worse" or "At least I've got my health." In this effort to look on the bright side, we succeed in cutting ourselves off from needed understanding and support.

Let's take Natasha's and Dan's circumstances off the table for a moment. Maybe it will be easier to see something of yourself in Kendra, whose suffering is far less dramatic although no less real. Kendra has her health, a loving husband and two children, and enough money to live comfortably. She feels she has no right whatsoever to complain about anything. Yet she's not happy.

For the past ten years, thirty-eight-year-old Kendra has been thinking of starting a business selling her handmade jewelry. Her husband supports the idea, but so far she hasn't done very much to get started. She feels trapped in what she considers a dead-end job as an office manager that takes up most of her time, most days each week. Evenings and weekends, she usually finds she has no energy to work on her business goal.

Kendra often feels bad about herself, especially when she doesn't feel like doing the things she knows she should as a budding entrepreneur—building a website, taking a class, or attending a networking event. She's also focused on what she sees as her pathological inability to get to the gym after work, even though she wants to be more fit.

Kendra's experiencing a serious lack of motivation. She knows what she "should" be doing, but she never seems to feel like doing it. The jewelry she's made in the past gathers dust in her garage. These days, she barely even feels like making new pieces, something that used to be fun and exciting for her.

Because she's *not* laid up in a hospital bed with traumatic injuries, Kendra tells herself she has "no excuse and zero tolerance" for not being more active. Her self-image sinks lower every year. The only solution she can think of is to push herself harder. "Just do it!," she urges herself. Sometimes this works for a little while. Other times, when she doesn't follow through, it just makes her feel worse.

Kendra isn't exactly alone in her predicament. She has a built-in drill sergeant. It's the insistent voice of her self-critical thoughts.

In real life, a drill sergeant is supposed to be tough; he or she is teaching people how to be soldiers. They need to learn skills that could mean the difference between life and death on the battlefield.

But Kendra's not a soldier. She's a civilian who lives in comparative safety. She doesn't need a drill sergeant yelling at her while she watches TV: "What do you think you're doing? You should be more pro-DUCK-tive!"

When she decides to stay home and read a book instead of attending a networking event, her inner drill sergeant screams, "You should be ashamed of yourself! What do you think this is? A pleasure cruise?!?"

When it's all just too much and Kendra's tears of frustration get the better of her, the drill sergeant is right there to ridicule and shame her: "My 98-year-old grandmother is tougher than you! Now stop your whining and get back out there!"

Kendra's drill sergeant has been with her so long, she doesn't remember when he first showed up. She doesn't even know what life would be like without this critical character.

She often wishes he'd go away, but, at the same time, she believes she needs him. Kendra doesn't realize that what would really motivate her is an inner caring friend instead of the harsh drill sergeant.

Kendra is so used to the critical tone of her own

thinking that it never occurs to her she might not deserve this harsh treatment. More to the point, the drill sergeant's yelling is not actually helping her accomplish her goals! It's just making her feel worse about herself, further sapping her motivation and energy.

Kendra has never imagined what it could be like to have an inner caring friend who says, "You're so tired; I can understand your desire to rest. Let me get you a pillow."

The very thought of such kindness fills Kendra with a confused tangle of emotions. There's relief and gratitude, but also fear and suspicion. What if she just allowed herself to rest whenever she wanted to? What if she let herself not do the things she should be doing, without criticizing herself?

No, she thinks, shaking her head as if to rid herself of an impure thought. If she were to "go soft" on herself, she'd never get anything done. She has to stay on her own case to keep that from happening. At least the inner drill sergeant will keep her from falling prey to enemies in the form of sadness, loneliness, regret, and despair. As long as she's at least *trying* to be productive, she's got something positive to focus on. She's got hope.

BE WHERE YOU ARE

"I believe that it may be normal, healthy, and even productive to experience mild to moderate depression from time to time as part of the variable emotional spectrum, either as an appropriate response to situations or as a way of turning inward and mentally chewing over problems to find solutions."

~ ANDREW WEIL, M.D.

"There is not a particle of life which does not bear poetry within it."

~ GUSTAVE FLAUBERT

"The emotion that can break your heart is sometimes the very one that heals it."

~ NICHOLAS SPARKS

"There is no object so foul that intense light will not make it beautiful."

~ RALPH WALDO EMERSON

"Our sweetest songs are those of saddest thought."

~ PERCY BYSSHE SHELLEY

"What good is the warmth of summer, without the cold of winter to give it sweetness?"

~ JOHN STEINBECK

"Oh, God of dust and rainbows, help us see that without the dust the rainbow would not be."

~ LANGSTON HUGHES

"If only we'd stop trying to be happy, we could have a pretty good time."

~ EDITH WHARTON

While Kendra's been trying to get herself to buck up and start her business, she's unaware that she's defying Nature itself. The fact is, Kendra has dysthymia (diss-THIGH-mee-uh), mild but chronic depression that can hang around for years. Depressed people don't start businesses. They don't go to the gym. They don't feel motivated to do much of anything.

Kendra's expecting way too much of herself in her present state. What she needs to do is address the problem inside before expecting results on the outside. She needs to accept her actual (rather than desired) experience, understand it, and allow herself to be pulled toward the next step rather than trying to push herself there.

Kendra is right to be hopeful that things can change, but she's looking for change in all the wrong places. She's trying to change her experience by *doing*, rather than by *being*.

Obviously, what she's been doing hasn't worked for her. Pushing herself to do things she doesn't feel like doing, bad-mouthing herself when she doesn't follow through... These actions have got her where she is today (which is nowhere she wants to be). She has nothing to lose by trying something totally and completely different.

What Does Wallowing Look Like?

There are things you're not supposed to do in company that seem okay to do when you're alone. I'm sure you can think of a few examples. Wallowing is one of those things. When you let yourself experience your true feelings, no one can see or hear what you're doing, so it's between just you and yourself. No one else can be offended, hurt, or disgusted by your thoughts and feelings. It's an even better deal than picking your nose, because you can't be caught doing it; wallowing is invisible and therefore totally private.

Here's a case in point. Picture yourself standing with a stranger at a cocktail party, having a polite chat, when the topic turns to pets. The stranger tells you that she pays a pet psychic to interpret her cat's dreams over the phone, and she's thrilled to announce that it turns out she and Foofoo were the king and queen of Arabia in a previous life. She wants to know if you have any pets that you used to be married to.

What do you feel? Are you intrigued? Irritated? Amused? Whatever you feel, you may decide to keep the full extent of it to yourself as you consider your reply.

Wallowing is like that. It's a private experience, something you're free to do in your own interior landscape, hurting no one.

That means that the rules that apply in company can be broken. For instance, while self-pity is socially awkward—even for people in Natasha's and Dan's positions—feeling sorry for yourself is perfectly safe and appropriate in the privacy of your own heart. You can even shout, "POOR ME!!!" inside your head. No one will be shocked because no one can hear what you say to yourself in your head.

With that understanding, let's see how Kendra might handle some typical unpleasant emotions if she wallows in her real feelings on an ordinary day.

Imagine that she's had some practice and gotten pretty good at it. Let's walk beside her in that internal landscape where thoughts and feelings intermingle. The following description will raise more questions about wallowing than it answers. Some of what you read may confuse or even alarm you; I promise to try to address your questions and concerns later. For now, just try to keep an open mind as you watch Kendra wallow like a pro.

> *Kendra's alarm startles her out of a deep sleep; she has to get up and get the kids ready for school. After dropping them off, she'll need to make her way to her own job, where she'll spend the next eight and a half hours. She told herself yesterday that no matter what happens, she has to go to the gym after work today, since she hasn't managed to get there all week and somehow it's already Thursday.*
>
> *What Kendra wants right now, as the clock radio barks a weather report, is to go back to sleep and stay that way indefinitely. It seems so unfair that she has to get out of bed!*
>
> *She acknowledges this truth to herself,*

silently saying and feeling, "I wish I could stay in bed forever." She becomes aware of a pitiful despair—she really doesn't want to get out of bed at all today, let alone right now—and so she purposely says to herself, "Poor me, I have to get up soon."

Kendra does herself the small kindness of hitting the "Snooze" button, allowing herself a few more precious minutes to doze. She wraps her arms around herself lovingly for good measure.

Note that she doesn't tell herself to buck up, doesn't berate herself for having stayed up so late. She just offers herself some sympathy.

At breakfast, she feels irritable. "I'm in a bad mood," she admits to herself. She focuses on doing only one thing at a time so as not to overburden herself this morning. She lets things that can slide, slide. She avoids criticizing herself for the way she feels.

Kendra doesn't evaluate her circumstances and ask herself whether she has any good reason to feel irritable. She knows that feelings always have their reasons, and there's no need to put herself on trial.

Still at home and getting ready for the day, Kendra allows herself to feel irritable instead of fighting it. She used to think she was a grouch when she felt this way. She doesn't call herself names anymore. Instead, she reflects to herself, "I'm irritable!" as often as she needs to, staying aware of her emotions as they ebb and flow. She knows she's a good person; being irritable doesn't make her bad.

Driving the kids to school with a big cup of coffee inside her, she notices she feels less irritable, more neutral, and even almost good despite the predictably heavy rush hour traffic. Being honest with herself about her mood has given her the space she needs to feel in control. It's a good feeling. As she completes the familiar trip to school, she thinks, "This is do-able."

Kendra didn't use positive thinking or distraction to change her feelings. They changed on their own with time. She knows that emotions, once felt, will always change. This gives her the confidence to roll with the feelings she has in any given moment.

The rest of her commute is uneventful. Kendra's not aware of any emotions in particular for the next few hours while she settles in at work and focuses on tackling the tasks of the day.

In the lunch room, she shares a laugh with a coworker, Jen, over an ad in the newspaper that promises, "Understand the meaning of your pet's dreams!" Kendra and Jen take turns thinking up anxiety dreams that dogs might have ("He's wearing clothes in public," or "He's scheduled for a flea exam and hasn't studied"), and Kendra thinks and feels, "This is nice. It feels so good to have a laugh. I enjoy my relationship with Jen."

Because she's aware of her inner life, Kendra can savor the moment and take in the simple pleasure of her friendship with Jen. If she hadn't learned to wallow, she might forget to enjoy this bright spot in her busy day.

In an afternoon meeting, Kendra's least favorite coworker, Dick, patronizes her and everyone else as usual. "I cannot stand this guy," she allows herself to think. "He bugs the [bleep] out of me!"

Kendra doesn't worry that her dislike of the man makes her a bad person. She knows that it's not necessary to like everyone in order to be a good person. It's all right for her to discriminate. She embraces her opinion and her feelings in the privacy of her mind.

All in all, the workday is an average one. Five-thirty comes, the Hour of Reckoning: Time for Kendra to decide whether to go to the gym.

"I just don't want to go. I'd love to let myself off the hook and go home instead," she thinks and feels as she shuts down her computer.

Sitting in her car outside the office, gym bag in the trunk, Kendra still doesn't want to go to the gym. She doesn't have another word for it, she just knows she feels bad. She says to herself, "I feel bad right now."

As she acknowledges what she's feeling, Kendra becomes aware that the only reason she's considering going to the gym is to avoid feeling like a failure. It's all about the outcome; if she goes, she'll feel good that she went, getting a temporary boost from her "good" behavior. If she doesn't go, she'll feel bad about herself. Again.

Kendra spells out her dilemma right there in the car. She tells herself, and feels, "I'm stuck. I don't want to go to the gym right now, but I'm afraid I'll feel bad about myself later if I don't."

She realizes that she's caught in a pattern of ignoring current feelings in favor of possible future feelings. Like right now. She'll feel such relief in this moment if she skips the gym, but she thinks she'll feel even better later if she goes, and much worse later if she doesn't.

But later doesn't always pan out the way it's supposed to, and any good feelings she gets from going to the gym now will last only a day or two. Then the cycle starts up again, with the same old struggle to get to the gym.

She lets the reality of the dilemma sink in, and she's surprised to find some compassion for herself emerge from the darkness. She's

*going to suffer either way. What a bum deal!
"This STINKS," she declares.*

*Suddenly, she doesn't feel so powerless.
She's having her feelings, they're not having
her. She feels better about herself. This is
a dilemma, pure and simple; whatever she
decides, she will both win something and lose
something.*

You might have noticed that I said very little about Kendra's behavior—how she interacted with others when she was having feelings. You might have wondered how she dealt with her husband and kids in her irritable mood, or whether she said anything to Dick or anyone else about his condescending behavior in the meeting, or what she decided to do about the gym.

I deliberately avoided discussing what Kendra did or didn't do, because I want to make the point that *how we feel* and *what we do* are two separate animals. I want you to get used to separating them in your mind. We'll revisit this distinction in Chapter 3, but for now, just know that the more room you allow for your emotions, the easier it will be to make good decisions about what to do.

If you were impressed by Kendra's ability to identify her feelings and motivations, rest assured it's a skill that can be acquired and developed with practice. Kendra did it, I've done it myself, and you can, too. This book will help you get started.

How to Use This Book

Constructive wallowing is like the perfect bikini wax, or passing a prostate exam; the results are worth the discomfort. But just like those procedures, giving yourself permission to wallow takes some courage. Reading this book will provide you with knowledge, examples, encouragement, and tools you can use to get to where you want to be. But you'll have to supply the determination to make it happen.

My experience with self-help books has been that they make me feel good when I'm reading them, but I don't usually do the activities they suggest. As long as I'm reading, I feel like I'm moving forward. But, once I finish the book, that feeling goes away. Then it's time to read another self-help book. Or eat ice cream.

Consider putting into practice what you learn as you move through the text. Or, if you find yourself just reading, as I do, keep the book handy once you've finished it. You never know when the mood to practice will strike, and when it does you'll be ready.

The material in the book builds on itself like a pyramid, with a broad base of essential concepts and a gradual honing and refining of them. It's best to read the book from start to finish, especially the first time through.

However, if you have specific questions or just prefer to jump around a bit, feel free to skip ahead to Chapter 7, "The Daunting Dozen: Top Twelve Wallowing Worries," and/or 9, "Wallowing Questions & Answers." Those chapters can be appreciated on their own. Just know that you'll have a better grasp of what's there once you've read everything that comes before.

In Chapter 1, you'll get a chance to find out how well your current strategy for dealing with emotions is working and establish a baseline to look back at later. You'll also see what happens when we suppress instead of embracing feelings. And we'll have a little chat about making time for your emotions.

In Chapter 2, I'll tell you something about my own wallowing journey and explain in a different way why it works so much better to make room for icky emotions instead of pushing them away.

After I lull you into a real(!) sense of security in Chapters 1 and 2, I'll get down to some slightly technical talk about emotions in Chapter 3, "Emotions: What You Don't Know *Can* Hurt You." Some people love this kind of nuts and bolts commentary, while others use it as a sleep aid; I've tried to make the section as lively as possible for both groups. It will serve a vital function, because you need to understand emotions if you're going to learn to trust them.

In Part II, comprising Chapters 4 through 6, I'll introduce you to the T-R-U-T-H Technique for constructive wallowing. I'll offer some encouragement and inspiration to give you confidence before you try the Technique for the first time. Once I've outlined the process, I'll provide examples. We'll see how Natasha from the Introduction is doing, among others, in using the Technique to address common emotional challenges. Of course, you'll also have room to practice the Technique yourself.

In the final chapters of the book that make up Part

III, we'll explore issues faced by people new to constructive wallowing, and I'll present some activities you can use to bulk up your wallowing muscles. Then I'll clarify and refine earlier material by answering common questions. Just before we look back and sum up our adventure together, you'll get a handy guide to choosing a therapist in case you'd like some personal support in embracing your new, feelings-friendly lifestyle.

At the end of each chapter you'll find a brief summary that captures key points in bullet form. These can help you find what you're looking for when you want to double back and reread something.

Every part of this book is designed to help you use your worst feelings to become your best self, so you can move forward with confidence and joy. As a bonus, you'll get back parts of yourself that you might have lost along the way. Reclaiming those parts will make you whole again, the way you were meant to be.

Summary

- Emotions make us whole.
- We met Vance, who thought he should be a robot.
- We met Natasha and Dan, who sustained life-changing injuries.
- Trying to look on the bright side cuts us off from compassion.
- Inner drill sergeants don't provide inspiration.
- We watched Kendra wallow.
- Good people feel all sorts of emotions, and don't necessarily like everybody.
- How we feel and what we do are two separate things.

PART I

Dip Your Toe in the Water

Chapter 1

Wallowing Is Mostly Allowing

I n the Introduction you met Vance, Natasha, Dan, and Kendra, who were all experiencing emotions in different life situations.

We saw how Vance tried to power through a breakup without missing a beat on his new job, and we watched Natasha reach for inspiring, positive words to fuel her journey back from the trauma of losing her ability to walk. Dan experienced every rotten feeling in the book, but came out on the other side. We left Kendra feeling vaguely unhappy with herself and looking for a way out of feeling stuck.

For all of us, how we deal with our feelings has an impact on how quickly we're able to bounce back from setbacks large and small.

How You Cope with Anything Is How You Cope with Everything

You may or may not have had an experience like Natasha or Dan, but, in any case, your life has *not* been all sunshine and lollipops. What do you do with difficult feelings when they come up from day to day, as you go about your life?

The following quiz will give you a sense of your relationship to your own emotions, and how that relationship is affecting your life and your outlook, for better or worse. It will give you a baseline as we get started, so that, at the end of our time together, you'll be able to look back and remember where you came from. The quiz is repeated in Chapter 8 for your convenience.

If you normally skip quizzes, I encourage you to pause here and do this one. Your answers may be different in this moment than they will be even a chapter or two down the road. You won't be able to go back in time to create a baseline.

I'll wait while you get a pencil. (Take your time; I've got a magazine and a snack.)

Okay, welcome back! How many of the following statements do you agree with? Don't think too hard about it; just go with your first impulse.

If you really aren't sure whether you agree or disagree, go with what your family would say. Scoring is explained on the next page. Try to avoid peeking!

Quiz

....

		Agree	*Disagree*

1. When bad things happen, I try to look on the bright side. _____ _____
2. I'd rather not see my friends when I'm unhappy. _____ _____
3. There's no sense in crying over something you can't change. _____ _____
4. I hate it when I get emotional over small things. _____ _____
5. Dwelling on negative feelings only makes them worse. _____ _____
6. I like to lead with my head, not my heart. _____ _____
7. Anger is a toxic emotion. _____ _____
8. I sometimes find my own feelings ridiculous. _____ _____
9. It's not healthy to let yourself dwell on negative feelings. _____ _____
10. I get annoyed at myself when I can't snap out of a funk. _____ _____
11. When I feel down, I try to think about things I'm grateful for. _____ _____
12. I shouldn't complain; other people have it worse than me. _____ _____
13. It's best not to think about things that make you upset. _____ _____

14. I often don't understand
    my feelings.   _____ _____
15. I can be pretty hard
    on myself.   _____ _____
16. I'm not comfortable
    with anger.   _____ _____
17. I'm not comfortable
    with tears.   _____ _____
18. I can be overly sensitive.   _____ _____
19. I feel anxious or depressed
    fairly often.   _____ _____
20. I should be able to control
    my emotions.   _____ _____

TOTALS: _____ _____

Scoring

Give yourself a point for every statement you agreed with. If you got creative and put a check mark somewhere between "Agree" and "Disagree," give yourself half a point.

In a nutshell, the more of the statements in the quiz you agreed with, the less likely you are to feel peaceful, centered, and content and the more trouble you're likely to have in relationships of all kinds, including the one with yourself.

If you agreed with zero to four of the statements above, congratulations! You're functioning very well because of the compassion and patience you express toward yourself and others. Your comfort with emotions helps you enjoy close relationships, and you probably have as many friends as you can handle. Focus on the statements you agreed with as you read the rest of this book; I'll try to talk you out of them.

Note: If this description doesn't seem to fit you, check to make sure you answered the questions accurately. Do you really *disagree* with that many of the statements?

If you agreed with five to nine of the statements, you have some positive feelings toward yourself, and you're generally functioning well, if inconsistently. Your self-compassion could use a tune-up. It's time to cut yourself some slack and enjoy the extra energy and good feelings you free up. Learning to wallow constructively will noticeably improve your qualify of life.

If you agreed with ten to fourteen of the statements, inner conflicts and injured self-esteem are likely keeping you from reaching your potential in relationships. Your happiness meter is not exactly zinging— life is grayer than it should be for you, at least in part because of the veil of self-criticism between you and the rest of the world. Use the tools and exercises in this book to help you focus on listening to your heart. Consider joining forces with a compassionate counselor or therapist as well.

A score of fifteen or more indicates a serious rift in your sense of well-being. You're probably exhausted just from keeping things together personally and/or professionally, even if you don't always let that show. Being close to other people may be scary for you, which makes relationships difficult. You need to take your own side more. If you don't believe you deserve compassion, take my word for it: You definitely do. Working with a counselor or therapist while you read through this book could be life-changing for you.

You might have noticed that I recommend counseling for those with very high scores. There's no particular cutoff score over which you should seek counseling, but, in general, the higher the score, the more you'll benefit from having someone with you in your corner modeling acceptance, patience, and compassion. For ideas on who that someone might be, see the Guide to Choosing a Therapist in Chapter 10.

If you scored nice and low, you still could benefit from working with a counselor. Finding the right match can help you move from "I'm fine" to "Wahoo! This is really living!"

Whatever your score, constructive wallowing can give you yourself, and your life, back. If you're ready to open your mind—and more importantly, your heart—to the idea that all emotions are acceptable (that's right, *all* emotions!), then let me wish you a very warm welcome to the path of self-acceptance. I'm honored to walk beside you.

Whatever worries you may have about letting yourself feel bad, I've had them too. I didn't always understand or trust that bad feelings weren't dangerous. I'll address specific "wallowing worries" in Chapter 7 and along the way there. But first, let me assure you that I understand if you agreed with any of the statements in that quiz back there. I think a little wordplay might shine some light here.

You Can't Wallow Unless You ALLOW

If you look at the word "wallow," you might notice that when you remove the first letter, "w," you end up with a whole new word: "allow." What a wonderful concept that is, and what a coincidence that out of a warthog of a word like "wallow" we can get such a beautiful and helpful new one.

ALLOW. Say that out loud and see if it doesn't make you breathe a little easier.

This handy lexical coincidence provides a way to remember what it means to (w)allow in feelings. It really just means that you're **allowing in** your true feelings. You're *allowing* them *in* to your awareness. You're allowing them to be what they are, without trying to change them. Allowing them just to be.

I'll use "(w)allow" and "wallow" interchangeably throughout this book to remind you of this deeper meaning.

It seems like a simple concept, allowing your feelings to exist. And yet it can also be confusing (Am I not already doing that? If not, how do I do it?) and frightening, too.

We don't necessarily trust our own emotions; they seem dangerous. Like a terrible monster trapped in a dungeon who sees a sudden opportunity for escape, bad feelings might explode outward if we open the door a crack, and wreak havoc in our lives.

I want you to know that (w)allowing in your feelings as described in this book is not only safe, it can change your life in two ways.

First, letting yourself have the feelings you have creates a more compassionate relationship between you and your emotions. Which is to say, between you and your authentic self. Your feelings are very much a part of you, and accepting your feelings as they are is the same as accepting yourself as you are.

So...

acceptance of feelings = self-acceptance

Constructive wallowing is the royal road to true and lasting self-acceptance.

Second, yucky feelings can only really leave us alone once we feel them fully. An unfelt feeling is trapped inside us just as surely as a rabbit in a cage with a combination lock. I'll explain this in much more detail later. The takeaway is that wallowing constructively in so-called negativity will enable you to get over said negativity faster and more surely than any other way, including positive thinking and using a gratitude journal. **Think about what a difference it could make in your life if you only had to deal with each feeling once instead of over and over again.**

When we refuse to (w)allow in "negative" feelings, what happens is that we push away the part of us that feels that way. This creates a fragmented self, with an Acceptable Me and an Unacceptable Me.

This fragmenting, in itself, is painful because it hurts when we don't feel whole. We came into this world whole and intact, and that's how we're meant to stay. When we're not whole, we miss ourselves.

In addition to rejecting parts of ourselves, when we refuse to (w)allow in our feelings we ensure that our worst feelings stay inside us longer than they need to. Emotions can't dissipate until we fully acknowledge and claim them. We'll talk much more later about why this is true, when we look at how feelings work.

For now, let me offer another equation, one you might be familiar with:

feeling = healing

You can either keep wrestling with your emotions and yourself, or you can accept yourself no matter how you feel. If you choose the latter, you'll not only experience the relief and delight of genuine self-acceptance, but you'll finally be able to truly "let go" of your stickiest emotions. This is how a person can use wallowing to work on healing even lifelong emotional pain.

We'll talk more about what it means to "let go" of a feeling later. Really letting feelings go the way that Nature intended—by wallowing in them—is a sure and simple path to self-acceptance and well-being.

If wallowing is so good for us, why do we resist it? Because of our negative association with certain emotions. We'll talk about "negative" feelings in different parts of the book (spoiler: there's no such thing).

I've heard from many people who worry that, if they allow themselves to fully let go and experience their "negative" emotions, they'll fall into a dark hole and never get out. If we write that belief as another equation, we might write:

wallowing in feelings = falling into a hole

Obviously, no one wants to have to claw their way back out of a hole full of bad feelings, or worse, get stuck down there forever. That's why we try so hard not to wallow in, let alone *have*, "negative" feelings. Have you ever found yourself whistling a cheery tune when you felt like crying, just to avoid that hole?

But wait a minute. What if that scary-looking hole is not what it appears to be? What if, instead of a dark dead end, it's a treasure chest holding your most authentic, powerful, and complete self?

If we take that "w" off the word "wallow" again, and stick it on to the front of the word "hole" in that last equation, we wind up with an interesting final thought:

__a__llowing in feelings = falling into a __w__hole

Now we've got that lovely word "allowing," and another equally beautiful word, "whole." There's a relationship between allowing ourselves to feel the way we do, and becoming whole. Simply put, when we allow our feelings into our awareness through wallowing in them, we move closer to being our true selves.

ON BECOMING WHOLE

"I've come to believe that all my past failure and frustration were actually laying the foundation for the understandings that have created the new level of living I now enjoy."

~ **ANTHONY ROBBINS**

"I have been bent and broken, but—I hope—into a better shape."

~ **CHARLES DICKENS**

"Pain or love or danger makes you real again...."

~ **JACK KEROUAC**

"Extraordinary people survive under the most terrible circumstances and they become more extraordinary because of it."

~ **ROBERTSON DAVIES**

"He knows not his own strength that hath not met adversity."

~ **BEN JONSON**

"The most beautiful people we have known are those who have known defeat, known suffering, known struggle, known loss, and have found their way out of the depths."

~ **ELISABETH KÜBLER-ROSS**

"We are like the herb which flourisheth most when trampled upon."

~ **SIR WALTER SCOTT**

"The aim of life is self-development. To realize one's nature perfectly—that is what each of us is here for."

~ **OSCAR WILDE**

Constructively wallowing in feelings, also known as having, embracing, witnessing, or tolerating feelings, leads us back to where we started out in life: with a fresh, clean slate.

(W)allowing puts us in touch with those parts of ourselves that are experiencing the feelings, including feelings that may have been with us for a very long time. When we make this connection to these lost parts of ourselves, we're like long-lost relatives reunited. Our hearts fill with love, longing, and connection.

Because I've personally gained so much from practicing constructive wallowing, I'm convinced that the way you and I were taught to deal with difficult emotions has done us more harm than good. I can't wait to share with you a different, more compassionate way to deal with all of your feelings for the rest of your life.

The Benefits of Wallowing

To be fair, let's start by listing reasons *not* to wallow. Here they are, as I understand them:

It seems to make things worse (i.e., more painful).

It feels wrong to embrace "negative" emotions.

It seems like it could lead to poor behavior.

It seems like it could lead to a loss of control.

It feels like you're a bad person if you feel "negative" feelings.

It seems weak.

It's easier not to.

None of the above is true. That's why I'm going to challenge every single one of those notions in this book. The real truth will set you free, and you'll never again be controlled by your emotions the way (dare I say?) you are now. You'll always have emotions. But having them is a far cry from being controlled by them.

You'll be surprised at what becomes possible when you make the simple change of allowing yourself to feel the way you do. Here are some of the areas where I've experienced improvement myself and either witnessed or heard about from others who practice embracing "negative" feelings:

- Self-acceptance
- Self-esteem
- Emotional health and well-being
- Closer relationships
- Confidence
- Mental clarity
- An end to constant worry
- Restful sleep
- Energy
- A larger capacity for relaxation, play, and joy

That's an impressive list, and I'm not even sure it's complete! Wallowing isn't a miracle cure or a quick fix. It's a common-sense mental adjustment that removes unnecessary emotional obstacles caused by bad habits. Those items on the list above all occur naturally in us unless something gets in the way. Wallowing respects Nature, which is always in flow and in flux. Just like our emotions.

I hope it's becoming clear that when we stop fighting our own feelings, we start to regain the pieces of ourselves we've been lonely for. The closer we are to being whole, the more inner resources we have to live our lives well, and to deal with the difficulties life inevitably brings our way.

The Escalation Cycle

When we ignore feelings, they get stuck inside us, and they multiply. You may be familiar with this escalation cycle in yourself or someone else. It goes like this:

You stuff (i.e., suppress) your feelings because they seem inappropriate, inconvenient, too painful, or too big for the circumstances. You might stuff them with food, alcohol, shopping, sex, or another activity that blankets your true emotional state with temporary good feelings. Or you might simply have trained yourself to ignore unpleasant feelings by not focusing on them. Either way, feelings get stuffed inside and the escalation cycle begins.

Escalation occurs because your stuffed feelings don't just go away. They pile up inside you until one of two things happens. Either the stuffed feelings explode outward, or they get buried deeper. Both outcomes erode your sense of well-being.

(The piling-up-inside-you thing is just a metaphor to describe a process in the brain no one fully understands, where memory gets involved in the emotional response and sensitivity is increased. But let's just imagine feelings piling up because that's easier to visualize, and the results are exactly the same regardless of how you think about the mechanism.)

Figure 1 shows the escalation cycle in action. Don't worry if the picture looks like the inside of a pasta-maker. I'll talk you through it. We can use Kendra from the Introduction as an example.

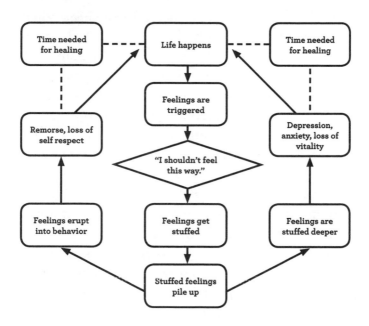

Figure 1. The Escalation Cycle

Figure 1 tells the story of how Kendra got to be where we first found her, lacking the motivation to start her jewelry business and suffering from mild depression while trying to force herself to go to the gym.

Let's begin at the top of the figure, in the middle, with "Life happens."

Feelings get triggered all the time; Forrest Gump's mother was right when she advised him, "Life is like a box of chocolates; you never know what you're going to get." You and I both know that life sometimes brings stuff that's more likely to hit a fan than be found in a box of chocolates. And, as life happens, so do feelings.

Almost every day, feelings large and small, good and bad, are triggered by normal life events. We can have feelings about everything from losing a job to losing a button, from finding a lump to finding a friend. Feelings are always there, ready to be triggered by what happens within and around us.

You might remember Kendra's self-pity over the fact that she couldn't stay in bed despite how nicely she was sleeping. Later in the day, her reactions to both her pleasant experience with humorous Jen in the lunch-room and her irritation with arrogant Dick in the staff meeting were two more sets of spontaneous feelings triggered when "life happened."

Everything up until now in Figure 1 is normal and natural; life happens, and feelings are triggered. The trouble starts with "I shouldn't feel this way."

Before she started practicing constructive wallowing, Kendra was used to trying to snap herself out of self-pity when it threatened to show its poor little face. Her occasional irritability was a source of shame. And her dislike of her condescending coworker was an ongoing thorn in her side, convincing her that she was mean-spirited because, gosh darn it, that darned Dick probably meant well. For years, Kendra argued with her feelings in this self-negating way, and stuffed them as a way to cope.

Once feelings are stuffed, as I said before, they have nowhere to go. They pile up on top of each other, adding mass to the growing, roiling heap until the pressure is too great to contain.

Eventually, the pileup of stuffed feelings is so great that one or, more often, both of two things will happen, as indicated in Figure 1 by the two arrows shooting out in different directions from "Stuffed feelings pile up" at the bottom of the diagram. From there, if we follow the arrow to the left, we arrive at "Feelings erupt into behavior," where emotions are acted out willy-nilly, usually in unpleasant behaviors that spew out of us like geysers. Emotions that aren't acknowledged tend to control us, rather than the other way around. The more we push them away and try not to notice them, the more powerful they become, to the extent that they can hijack our behavior.

After such an eruption, there's some relief of the internal pressure of all those pent-up feelings, but there's also remorse for what's usually *not* our best behavior. That's how we arrive at the "Remorse, loss of self-respect" part of the diagram.

Kendra wasn't given to eruptions in the form of angry outbursts or violent behavior, but, when her irritability got the better of her, she would find herself sniping at her husband and losing patience with the kids. She would get angry at herself for this, and angry at them for irritating her, all of which made her doubt her goodness. This is the consequence of the left (explosive) side of the escalation cycle.

Meanwhile, Kendra was also a champion stuffer; what didn't come out in irritability got stuffed deeper, adding weight to a sinking ship. Like many people, Kendra didn't live exclusively on one side or the other of the escalation cycle; she both erupted and stuffed deeper to manage piled-up feelings.

Since the pre-wallowing Kendra preferred to suppress unpleasant feelings when possible, rather than erupting freely as some people seem to do, she experienced the loss of vitality typical of the right (depressive) side of the escalation cycle diagram. This includes lack of motivation, loss of initiative, and a grayed-out sense of identity. Her obsession with getting to the gym may have been fueled by anxiety, another common byproduct of stuffed feelings. (By the way, you can read more about anxiety in Chapter 9's Q&A section).

Suppressed feelings can cause chronic emotional and possibly even physical pain for the stuffer. You can probably attest to that if you tend to stuff your feelings. To make matters worse, life keeps happening and feelings keep getting triggered, whether you're ready for another round or not. The "Time needed for healing" shown in the top corners of Figure 1 seems like a luxury. That's why it's usually bypassed, as indicated by the dotted lines.

How can a full-time parent, employee, home-maker, caregiver, student, performer, traveler, business owner, or just about anyone other than an infant take the time in this fast-paced world to slow down and get off this crummy-go-round? I'll give you some ideas in the "When to Wallow" section below. But first, are you ready for a piece of good news?

There is a way out of the Escalation Cycle, and that is to step into the Constructive Wallowing Cycle instead. (See Figure 2.) By wallowing in your emotions, you facilitate their moving through instead of getting stuck inside you. It's like letting off steam; it reduces internal pressure.

"Letting off steam" is a phrase used for some pretty extreme activities, like yelling, driving fast, beating people up, and other exercises that burn fuel. But you can let off steam quietly and privately just by allowing yourself to experience your emotions. No need for extra fuel—and, actually, you'll *gain* fuel by letting your feelings roam free inside your heart and mind.

Suppressing feelings takes energy. Once you trust your feelings enough not to stuff them, you'll get that energy back for other things.

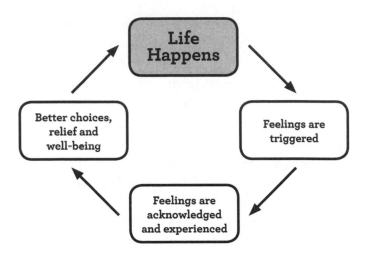

Figure 2. The Constructive Wallowing Cycle

Notice that the two eternal truths—"Life happens" and "Feelings are triggered"—remain the same as in Figure 1 at the start of the cycle. But instead of being stuffed and allowed to pile up, feelings are acknowledged and embraced as soon after they happen as possible. (See bottom of Figure 2.) This leads to relief of any internal emotional pressure and the release of any energy previously used to suppress emotions.

Acknowledging and experiencing feelings also necessarily allows them into conscious awareness, where we can keep an eye on them; they can be considered but not necessarily obeyed, resulting in better choices and, overall, a greater sense of wholeness and well-being.

Kendra is learning to consciously experience, tolerate, and accept all her feelings. You heard her doing exactly that as we followed her through her day in the Introduction. Instead of pushing past her morning irritation or trying to ignore it, which might have led to an outburst, she acknowledged how she felt and chose to slow down her morning activities (concentrating on doing just one thing at a time) in response. Instead of pushing away her mood to make room for life's activities, she changed her activities to make room for her mood.

As you can see, the problem of suppressed or explosive, out-of-control feelings can't happen if the Escalation Cycle is interrupted. Wallowing gives us a way to do that. It's a concrete alternative we can practice right away.

The rest of this book will illuminate the healing and productive process of embracing feelings. It's simple, and yet it can be hard to grasp in practical terms. The most frequently asked question about wallowing is, "Now that I've acknowledged the feeling, what do I *do* with it?"

It might take a couple of episodes of wallowing well to really *grok* the following truth: You don't have to do anything at all with a feeling; it's already doing something with you. Once you become conscious of the fact that you're having a feeling, and you refuse to fight with that feeling, you're no longer in the same place you were in the moment before. You've changed. Things are moving right along. All there is to *do* is to let the change that wants to happen, happen.

Constructive wallowing is like those *Magic Eye* books that were so popular in the 1990s. On each page there's nothing but a colorful pattern made of dots of ink.

Sort of pretty, but mostly a so-what kind of thing. *Until...* If you stare at each page long enough, relaxing your eyes and your mind, then at some point beyond your conscious control, a three-dimensional picture suddenly emerges from the pattern. It's breathtaking, especially the first time it happens! Once the picture gels in your brain, it's easier to find it the next time you try.

I'll present the dots of constructive wallowing from different angles throughout this book until the picture becomes clear. Once you see it, you won't be able not to.

Finding Time to Wallow

Wallowing is like brushing your teeth; it's a great thing to do, but not in the middle of a job interview. Certain times are more appropriate than others for even the healthiest of activities. It's ideal to have at least a little bit of "down time" to devote to wallowing so you don't get distracted. Almost everybody has some free time in their schedule if they look for it, but of course, your schedule is unique to you. Look for down time between obligations. If you have *zero* free time in your life, well, um... You might ask yourself why the president of the United States has free time and you don't!

If you're feeling stuck and/or emotional, pretty much the only constructive use of your time is to pay attention to your emotions. They're not going to let you go until you do. In this sense, you don't have time *not* to wallow.

Our lives are so full nowadays, we have to make appointments with ourselves just to take a shower. (Or is that just me?) But all is not lost if you're extremely busy. Like Kendra, whose day we followed in the Introduction, you can wallow a little in the emotions of the moment as you go about your life. All you need to do is be honest with yourself about how you feel. This might take a lot of practice, *not* because you're a big liar, but because maybe you're not used to paying attention to your feelings in a curious, rather than criticizing, way.

Or at all.

Also, you might not have enough feeling words in your vocabulary yet, and your feelings are a moving target. That makes it double-hard to pin them down in words. Don't worry; we'll take care of that later. A little bit of wallowing, even five minutes, is better than never wallowing at all.

Take a few minutes to pay attention to your feelings when you're:

- Standing in line
- Walking to or from the car
- Using the bathroom
- On hold
- Stopped in traffic
- At the airport
- In a waiting room
- Doing housework

If you can make a regular time in your schedule, and if you like to stay active, you can combine wallowing with exercise. In particular, anger is an emotion that lends itself to movement. Running, boxing, kick-boxing, or any other aerobic activity is fantastic.

I'm a big fan of walking, so I wallow in small upsets sometimes when I walk. I silently ask myself what's bothering me and try to describe what I'm feeling, and I open myself to experiencing the feeling as I stroll. Bigger issues usually find me wallowing at home when I don't have to be anywhere for a while, and where I can enjoy the support of my partner, Mike.

Space can also be an issue. Unless you live alone, you might want to find a place to wallow either privately, in a support group designed for that purpose, or one-on-one with a good friend or a compassionate therapist.

I have clients who tell me that the car is their favorite place to feel their feelings, especially if they have a long commute. They like the perceived isolation and privacy of solo driving. Coincidentally, the car is where I first learned to wallow myself, as I'll explain in the next chapter.

You don't have to wallow alone if you don't want to, but it's tremendously important that anyone present be comfortable with emotion. You also need to be totally comfortable with that person's being there. If there's any discomfort on either side, your wallowing won't be productive. If you're not sure, do it alone. You have some control over your own reaction to your feelings, but none whatsoever over anyone else's. Fearful, chiding, scornful, mocking, or absent reactions to your feelings are what alienated you from yourself in the first place; protect yourself from these influences until you've healed from the wounds they inflicted.

And speaking of mocking and chiding, be kind and understanding in your self-talk as you go about your busy day. Make sure the words you direct at yourself in your head are supportive rather than critical. This will lay the groundwork for safely feeling your emotions when you have more time to devote to wallowing in them.

There are admittedly times in life when a wee bit of wallowing is not going to be enough to help you dig out from under a mess of strong feelings. When should you deal with those bigger emotions, ones that are either old, jumbled, intense, or all of the above? If you're not finding enough time or space to be with your feelings during your normal routine, take a vacation. Go somewhere alone and take this book, your journal, and a box of tissues with you. Claim your time and space by taking it.

Summary

- Wallowing is mostly allowing (and other wordplay).
- Accepting feelings is a form of self-acceptance.
- Feelings are what make us whole.
- Suppressing emotions causes them to escalate, creating depression and anxiety.
- We talked about the Escalation and Constructive Wallowing cycles.
- Make time for wallowing whenever your schedule allows.
- A little bit of wallowing is better than none at all.

Chapter 2

The Accidental Wallower: My Story

M any years ago, long before I could even *spell* the
word "psychotherapy," let alone had any experience with it, I stumbled on the therapeutic power of
wallowing while driving on a Los Angeles freeway. No
one was hurt in the process, I'm happy to say!

In my mid-twenties, I was nurturing a dream of
becoming an actress, mostly because I wanted a job that
didn't feel like work or require me to wear a uniform. If
I'd known I could achieve those aims as a counselor in
private practice, I could have gone right back to school
and saved myself a bundle on headshots.

Anyway, there I was in 1995, living in Hollywood,
following the dream. But driving home from acting
class one day, I was not happy.

I was thinking about a young woman in my class

who was not only a talented actress, but also smart, funny, utterly charming, and easily twice as pretty as me. She was seriously cramping my style; I wanted to be the best actress, the "phenom," in that class. She was upstaging me just by being there. Her hair had more talent than I did. I was miserable.

The acting teacher, on whose opinion I'd hung my career hopes and dreams, seemed to delight in her, while being apparently incapable of remembering my name even after three months of weekly classes. Compared to her, I felt as exciting as a fake fern. How was I supposed to "wow" the producers in the movie biz if my own acting teacher looked right through me?

As I drove home from class that day, I was aware of vaguely "icky" emotions trying to rise up inside me. I didn't exactly know what I was feeling, I just knew it was bad. I didn't want to feel bothered by the situation in acting class. But I *was* bothered.

I tried distracting myself by turning on the radio, but that didn't work. I still felt awful, and I couldn't find anything I liked, so I turned it off.

Unpleasant memories sprouted in my mind: The enthusiastic applause for the Other Woman's scenes, compared to the lukewarm reception of mine; the teacher's warm smile and high praise for her, and his distracted, more critical comments to me.

I pushed the bad feelings away, but they didn't get the message; they hung around and kept pestering me while I drove. They were there whether I wanted them to be there or not.

Spontaneously, I decided to speak my feelings aloud.

There I was in my car, sitting in traffic—this was before everyone had cell phones, let alone hands-free devices for the car—speaking to no one.

"I'm jealous," I said.

There. It was out of the bag.

Nothing bad happened, so I said it again.

"I'm so *jealous*," I said, with some curiosity about where this was going, but also with more heat this time. "I'm jealous of her and her talent and good looks. I'm jealous because the teacher thinks she's brilliant and thinks nothing of me!"

I was on a roll now—as bizarre as it sounds, this was starting to feel kind of good, just saying exactly what I felt. "I hate that she's the teacher's pet. I hate that I feel like chopped liver in that class. I want what she has. *I'm so jealous of her!*"

Well, imagine my surprise when I discovered that I felt not worse, but better! The poison inside me was gone for the moment. While I'd been wrestling with those painful feelings, I felt toxic. But once I stopped fighting and just acknowledged them, I felt cleaner.

And then there was another weird surprise. The next feeling that came to me was actually *affection* for this Other Woman. She was, after all, a genuinely nice person with a cheeky sense of humor, who had made overtures of friendship to me (which I'm sure I'd rebuffed because of my insecurities).

It was as if, by claiming all of my stinky feelings about the situation, I'd made room for all my other feelings, including a very real appreciation for this charming budding actress.

It turns out that's not really too surprising. Later we'll talk about how feelings are like a cloud of trapped butterflies—it's hard to let one out without accidentally freeing a few others.

I was flabbergasted by how much relief it brought for me just to accept how I felt. And shocked that I ended up feeling friendly toward a woman whom I'd thought of as Public Enemy Number One just a short while earlier.

I didn't feel the need to tell her about my feelings, but I wasn't going to lie to myself anymore. I felt jealous and small in that class. That was the truth. And in a very real and practical sense, it set me free.

I was able to see clearly for the first time how important the teacher's approval was to me, especially since I was using his attitude to measure my chances of success as an actress. I understood why I felt so jealous of my classmate; she had something that was terribly important to me. The picture of the situation that I held in my mind became clearer, more nuanced, and less threatening.

Does that mean the difficult feelings went away? No. They lost much of their force, but they didn't stop coming up until the class was over. Until then, the situation remained the same; the teacher continued to go back and forth between apathy and criticism toward my work, while evidently being enchanted with everything my classmate did. The situation was inherently painful. The difference that wallowing made was, **the actual feelings were manageable in a way that lying to myself about them was not.**

With my emotions out of the bag, ironically, they

felt more under control. I had chosen to own them; they didn't own me anymore.

The talented classmate and I became acting class buddies. We'd sit together, do scenes together and gossip about what happened in class and beyond. In the end, because of her, I looked forward to being there.

I didn't completely stop being jealous of her. It's just that it became okay with me if I felt jealous. It was only a feeling; it didn't have to be a policy. There was nothing I needed to do about it. I certainly didn't have to struggle against it.

I had to wallow in my feelings to help my jealousy integrate with the rest of me. Not to do so would have meant stuffing that jealousy down deep inside my heart somewhere, where it would remain and create a vague sense of "yuck," keeping me from not only being happy, but enjoying a new friendship.

I had spontaneously wallowed, and it had been constructive. And all because of a random decision to stop fighting with myself and just go with what I was feeling for a moment. It's a good thing I'm insecure and petty, or this book might not have been written!

I long ago lost touch with my talented friend. A recent Internet search for TV, film, or theater acting credits under her name turned up nothing at all, but I did find a photo of a beautiful real estate agent with a cheeky smile full of confidence. I'm not sure it was her. But I suspect she went into something that doesn't feel like work to her, or require her to wear a uniform.

Getting Over a Happy Childhood

A short time after my impromptu wallowing session in the car, I moved from Los Angeles to New York City to continue pursuing an acting career, and to find an acting teacher who might remember my name.

Within a year of landing at La Guardia airport on a steamy July day, I was lucky enough to bag a day job as an in-house temp, and later an associate producer, for a very successful cable TV network. Somehow I also came up with enough apartment-finding mojo to snag an affordable one-bedroom apartment in Greenwich Village.

It didn't take me long to learn that if you had a cool, creative job in television and wanted to fit in, you needed to get into therapy. (This was especially true if you were also pursuing an acting career, since you were obviously crazy.)

The idea of therapy intrigued me. I had questions as I turned thirty. Who was I? Was acting really my true calling? And if so, should I get new headshots?

I discovered that there were approximately as many therapists in Manhattan as pigeons, and it wasn't hard to find one (a therapist, not a pigeon) through a friend. It was actually mostly a lark; I didn't really believe I needed therapy. I thought I was just following the maxim, "When in New York, do as New Yorkers do." I had no way of knowing that entering therapy would change the course of my career and my life.

I'm glad to say that the wonderful and gifted therapist I ended up working with was what I call "feelings-friendly." I'll describe what I mean by that in a moment.

A good therapist (i.e., a counselor, clinical psychologist, clinical social worker, or other mental health professional) can be a powerful ally in wallowing constructively. I was fortunate to find a great support in my therapist, Denise, without even knowing what to look for. The majority of therapists are feelings-friendly, at least in theory, so the odds were in my favor, much as they are for you today. Still, I offer you a guide to choosing a therapist in Chapter 10.

I went into therapy thinking I'd had a Happy Childhood and a perfectly fine life up till that point. And you know what? I was absolutely right. What I didn't realize was what that meant. Like the high-functioning clients I now see in my own practice, I'd survived numerous emotional injuries in my life that I hadn't ever fully acknowledged. Ours is a culture that champions the Survivor, not the Victim. If something hurts you, you're supposed to shake it off, especially if it's not a big deal as far as others are concerned. Like many other people, I learned that lesson young. It's extremely rare not to.

In *The Drama of the Gifted Child,* Alice Miller relates a scene observed on a walk, involving ice cream, a toddler, and two loving parents who know better than to hand an entire bar of ice cream to a two-year-old. They share their ice cream with him, but he's frustrated; he wants his own. The parents find his reaction amusing, and affectionately try to demonstrate that it's not a big deal. See? He can have a bite of theirs. In the end, the boy gets to hold the stick left over from his dad's ice cream which, predictably, he finds disappointing. Miller explores the boy's emotional response to his parents' unwittingly callous denial of his desire for autonomy and mastery. He feels humiliated, miserable, and alone compared to his parents. To him the ice cream *is* a big deal. Presumably, he stops thinking about it pretty quickly once the scene is over, but that momentary frustration and humiliation will happen hundreds more times during what he'll look back on as his Happy Childhood.

Just as with its opposite, the Happy Childhood provides children with more than enough training in suppressing emotions, and in getting back up without a fuss when they've been knocked down. While these skills can be useful, the lessons that give rise to them also do damage to children's emotional literacy. (See Chapter 3, "Emotions: What You Don't Know *Can* Hurt You.")

LESSONS FROM THE SCHOOL OF HARD KNOCKS

"We face up to awful things because we can't go around them, or forget them. The sooner you say 'Yes, it happened, and there's nothing I can do about it,' the sooner you can get on with your own life."

~ E. ANNIE PROULX

"There are some things you learn best in calm, and some in storm."

~ WILLA CATHER

"The real glory is being knocked to your knees and then coming back. That's real glory. That's the essence of it."

~ VINCE LOMBARDI, JR.

"You can't be brave if you've only had wonderful things happen to you."

~ MARY TYLER MOORE

"Do you not see how necessary a world of pains and troubles is to school an intelligence and make it a soul?"

~ JOHN KEATS

"Maybe it *did* take a crisis to get to know yourself; maybe you needed to get whacked hard by life before you understood what you wanted out of it."

~ JODI PICOULT

"The roughest roads often lead to the top."

~ CHRISTINA AGUILERA

"In three words I can sum up everything I've learned about life: it goes on."

~ ROBERT FROST

How painful these lessons are can vary. Every family has its own rules about what to do with feelings, including which emotions can be expressed, and how, and by whom. In my own case, there was very little talk about feelings in the family. Like, virtually none. The only emotions I recall being on display at home were anger and amusement. These feelings weren't named or discussed, but it was okay for all of us to express them. If we were angry, we shouted at each other. Not ideal, but arguably better than stuffing the anger. In my home, anger didn't get physical, nor verbally abusive. No one was called nasty names or told they were useless. Every one of us had a right to express anger, no one was assaulted, and our relationships weren't damaged irreparably. We tolerated each other's outbursts, and I learned that being angry isn't inherently dangerous.

My experience since then has been that this open and non-threatening (though not necessarily effective or polite) expression of anger isn't the norm. Most of the people I talk with come from families that either didn't show anger or expressed it in frightening ways. The common conception of anger as a "toxic" emotion is understandable when you think about how badly it's handled by almost everyone.

Amusement was the only other acceptable emotion in my house, and that was fun and easy to tolerate. We were able to laugh and be playful with each other. Ribbing was allowed and tolerated by all...with the help of suppressing any hurt feelings that might result.

There was no vocabulary, verbal or otherwise, for vulnerable feelings like hurt, sadness, loneliness, regret, disappointment, or fear. So I learned to hide those feelings from both others and myself. They seemed somehow shameful. It was best to ignore them.

Rejecting those feelings was a good strategy, at least at first. Who wants to feel those things, anyway? Feh! But the strategy was a little hard to follow when something *did* hurt. What was I to do with my pain?

I was only five years old the first time I remember actively stuffing a feeling. My family was fishing at a game farm, and my dad had snagged a fish. Excitement! My mom, my brother, and I gathered round, eager to watch him land it. I remember wanting to help my dad pull in the fish. I must have put my hands on the fishing pole, because he pushed me away with a barked instruction to stay clear. I was deeply shocked and hurt. I couldn't understand why my dad would push me away when I just wanted to help him. I remember having the thought that it wouldn't be good to cry, and so I didn't. I swallowed my tears so hard, it hurt my throat. For me, that particular family outing was ruined. I wanted to cry and cry, but we didn't do that in my family. Even though we loved each other, no one quite knew what to do about tears. So instead I endured an aching throat, full of squelched anguish, for what seemed like hours afterwards.

As I grew older, I stuffed away enough vulnerable feelings that my self-esteem was affected. I was full of barely acknowledged but highly shameful feelings; how could my self-esteem not be deflated by all that embarrassing cargo?

Getting hurt emotionally seems to be part of

growing up, and it's certainly a part of living. Some of us are injured more often or more deeply than others, but, as my therapist Denise used to say, and now I say to my own clients, "Pain is pain." There's no need to make comparisons.

There's a catalog of human experience that we all understand, including:

- occasional or frequent criticism or neglect from our all-too-human parents
- the cruelty of other children when we're young
- teachers and, later, bosses who make our lives miserable
- betrayals, large and small, by friends and lovers
- everyday and exceptional failures and losses
- experiences that frighten us and shake our sense of safety in the world
- etc., etc., etc.

The list is long.

Apart from my experience in the car a few years earlier, the idea that it's okay to look at these hurts and fully acknowledge them was totally new to me when I started therapy. It was an awakening. I'd entered therapy on a whim. I was just there to look around, and I didn't anticipate how much there would be to see.

As Denise listened to me talk about my life, she simply pointed to the emotions I didn't even realize I had, and helped me name them. She never suggested that my feelings were mistaken, or that I should try to get over them. Rather, she helped me make sense of why my emotions were as they were, and assured me that it was fine for them to be there. That is to say, she was friendly to my feelings. Hence the term "feelings-friendly."

You might be thinking, "Aren't therapists supposed to help clients feel *better*, instead of just accepting the fact that they feel bad?"

Good question. First, I did feel better just knowing that my feelings were acceptable and made sense. But it didn't stop there. **Once I could accept my feelings as they were, *they changed*.**

This is the healing paradox of wallowing in rotten feelings. You've got to accept what is, or else be stuck with it. Once you decide to just be where you are, you'll soon find yourself somewhere else.

Here's an analogy that might help clarify this. Let's say you're walking over the Brooklyn Bridge toward Manhattan. All's going well until you find yourself in the middle of the bridge. Suddenly, you can't stand walking on this bridge for even one more step. You feel like you've been walking toward Manhattan long enough. Now you just want to be there.

If you stand still and refuse to continue walking, you'll never get to where you want to be. You've got to keep doing what you're doing and trust that it will eventually get you to where you want to be. If you really hunker down and accept the task of walking, the bridge will be behind you before you know it.

In my own therapy, I saw this principle in action time after time. Just when I'd accepted where I was, I'd find myself somewhere new. Feelings are not designed to hang around forever; once you feel them, they dissipate. That leaves room for the next experience. And embracing that one leaves room for the one after it. And so on.

I learned to (w)allow in not just current hurts but in older feelings, too. I came to see that these are often related; today's hurt can piggy-back on yesterday's, creating a big reaction to a small event.

That combination of old and new injuries turned a molehill into an emotional mountain for me, complete with an eruption of tears, thirty years after my dad rejected my attempt to help him catch a fish. One morning, when I was working in a large office, a coworker I felt close to met my warm, happy greeting with outright hostility. I was stunned. It took work on my part to get her to talk to me about what was going on. When she finally did, I learned that when I'd said, "Hey! Great to see you," she thought I was purposely broadcasting her late arrival to everyone in the vicinity. I hadn't even realized she'd arrived late. I was so devastated by her contemptuous and unfathomable interpretation of my motives that I couldn't help spilling some tears on the shoulder of another (thankfully very kind and understanding) coworker. That theme of offering something of myself and having it roughly slapped away is one that I've been sensitive to since the fishing incident. That deep old hurt hitches a ride on fresh new ones, and the more closely the theme of the new incident matches the original one, the stronger my feelings are. That day in the office, I cried some of the tears I'd swallowed when I was five.

Learning this simple fact, that emotions tie back to

earlier events and make small deals feel like big ones, helped me make sense of my experiences, my feelings, and myself. Which made me feel better and stronger overall.

Though I was often surprised and pained by unpleasant feelings that came up in the course of therapy, Denise seemed convinced that nothing was wrong with me. The fact that one of us was okay with my having "negative" feelings gave me confidence that feelings—no matter how ugly or hard to bear—are not as dangerous as I'd thought.

My therapy quickly went from casual curiosity to serious work, as deep, old feelings bubbled up to the surface, caught by current events in my life in New York. These clamored to be explored in an emotionally safe environment. As I (w)allowed in the feelings old and new, I was working my way through an emotional backlog that had built up for years. Even with a Happy Childhood and thirty years of a relatively pleasant existence, I had work to do to step into wholeness and joy.

There's no point in feeling guilty if you think you've had a good life but you still aren't happy. You're not on this earth to be just okay or satisfied with not being traumatized. I'm assuming you're here to have a wonderful experience and meet your potential as a unique human being. Claiming and embracing your pain is necessary for living an optimal life. And if you don't have pain, you haven't been paying attention.

I knew I was the stereotypical privileged white woman when I sought counseling. But I caught on quickly to the fact that, as lucky as I was in many ways,

I hadn't always had the room, or given myself the time, or had the confidence, to fully process important feelings—particularly the "negative" ones that are no fun to have. I was functioning, but I wasn't living optimally.

It was as if all my minor but unfelt bad feelings had backed up inside me, ready to spring forth at the first sign of an opening. Not only was I emotionally constipated, but as I've said, I was not a whole person. Too much of me was tied up in those "stuck" feelings in the backlog.

Now remember, this whole backlog thing is a metaphor. I don't mean that there's a physical backlog of emotion trapped in a particular place inside your body... unless there is.

Many interesting books have been written about the relationship between emotions and physical health. If it makes sense to you to think of stuck feelings existing either physically, energetically, or in some other way inside your body, so be it. But if you don't believe in a literal emotional backlog, that doesn't matter. Just think of the word "backlog" as a reminder of what needs to happen in order for you to take control of your emotional life. A backlog needs to be cleared before things can get moving again the way they're supposed to.

You may be a do-it-yourself type, but for me, therapy provided a safe and convenient place to let my painful and/or confusing feelings have their day. All they needed was to move through me on their way out; I had to experience them. Not talk about them. Not think about them. *Feel* them. And that's what I learned to do.

Was it painful? Yes. Was it worth it? Double yes!

In feeling all the emotions that came into my awareness, I reconnected with myself in a way I didn't even know I needed to. The result was that after wallowing regularly for a short while I developed more confidence and ease. Not being whole had made me feel insecure; moving toward wholeness allowed me to be more comfortable in my own skin.

Nowadays, while offering kindness or help and being rebuffed in response is still a tender spot for me, it feels more about the other person's mood than about me, and I'm no longer prone to uncontrollable tears when it happens.

The work continues, as it always will. It took me years to make real headway on my emotional backlog, and there's always a new feeling in bloom, needing my attention. I'm no emotional genius; I often think I'm feeling irritable when I'm really just thirsty. But what I lack in clarity I make up for in emotional courage and self-compassion. I'm comfortable with feelings. I don't suffer from chronic anxiety or depression. I have energy to pursue my relationships, my hobbies, and my life's work. These are the payoffs of wallowing.

Ditch That Backlog!

Clearing an emotional backlog is a little like scooping water out of a rowboat that has a small leak in the bottom. As long as your bucket removes more water than the hole is letting in, you'll manage to keep the boat afloat.

But bailing does take time and effort, especially when you start out with the boat already half-full of water.

After a while, to continue with the analogy, you've cleared out most of the water and the boat's no longer in danger of sinking. You'll still need to do some bailing occasionally, but you can do it in a more leisurely way. You've got the tool and the time.

As far back as my accidental wallowing session in the car all those years ago, in which I spontaneously experienced the power of being honest with myself about my feelings, the wallowing technique I'll introduce you to in Part II was beginning to take shape. Knowing and naming feelings, which we'll discuss in the next chapter, are the first two parts of the process.

In order to heal and soothe difficult feelings, it's necessary to be not only honest but kind and gentle. Not as a luxury, but out of necessity if you're serious about healing. Self-compassion is built right into the technique I'll teach you, in the form of uncovering self-criticism and replacing it with self-acceptance and understanding.

But even honesty and kindness can't heal fully on their own. There's another crucial element required—a potentially scary one. And that is simply to *feel*.

If you're worried that wallowing just means making yourself feel worse in addition to wasting time, your concern is understandable. It doesn't seem to make any sense to wallow in the very feelings you wish you didn't have to begin with.

That's why in the next chapter you'll become an expert on how emotions work, and how they don't. You may be surprised to find that at least some of what you believe about feelings is a big fat myth.

You'll really get, for example, why the more you try to "let go" of an emotion, the more it sticks to you like discarded gum on your shoe. I'll tell you how to actually let emotions go, and I'll give you some good reasons to feel better about yourself while you're at it.

Our first stop will be to examine common terms. We've got to know what we're referring to if we're going to talk about feelings. Not everyone shares the same language, and many people like me didn't learn feeling words when we were growing up.

Imagine if you didn't know the words for different foods. All you could say was "I ate something good" or "I ate something bad." It would be hard to tell anyone what you wanted to eat without handy shortcuts like "taco," "grapefruit," or "fondue." You wouldn't be able to describe a meal you had. You might recognize it if you saw it again but you'd have quite a job describing a whole meal without any food-words. You'd also have no idea what to say if someone offered you a shiitake-mushroom-and-gruyère omelet. A *what,* now?

Language and words help us to organize our ideas so we can think clearly about things. We make sense of the world around us, and within us, through language. That's why you'll get a crash course on feeling words in Chapter 3 whether you need it or not.

To the extent that there's been any outdated, confused, or rigid thinking in your life about emotions, I bet you'll find the next chapter both freeing and thought-provoking.

Summary

- I told you my story.
- Even a happy childhood yields emotional injuries.
- Emotions that aren't fully experienced create a backlog that must be worked through in order to be released.
- Feeling your emotions helps to clear the backlog, like bailing out a boat.

Chapter 3

Emotions:
What You Don't Know *Can* Hurt You

You may have heard this pun before: *When the butcher backed into the meat grinder, he got a little behind in his work.*

Double meanings can be funny, but they can also cause unnecessary confusion when we're trying to talk seriously about things. So before we go any further, let me clarify some of the words I use frequently in this book. Because even though having feelings is something we all understand, talking about them can be confusing.

Feelings vs. Emotions

Feelings are sensations we're aware of. Feelings can be physical, meaning we experience them as happening in the body. Numbness, tingling, pain, an itch, goose bumps, etc.—these are all examples of physical feelings. We won't talk much about these since we're focusing on the other kinds of feelings in this book.

Feelings that aren't physical are called emotions. You can think of these as mental or spiritual feelings, or just plain "Feelings" as in the song by that name ("Feelings, nothing more than feelings, trying to forget my feelings of love..."). Joy, frustration, gratitude, and despair are all examples of feelings that are also emotions.

Some people make a distinction between them, but you may have noticed that in this book I use the words "feeling" and "emotion" to mean the same thing. Whenever I say "feelings" you can substitute the word "emotions," and vice versa.

"Negative" Emotions

What's a negative emotion? I'd like you to consider the idea that there's no such thing.

For our purposes, emotions are like your toes. They're exactly what they are—the way that Nature intended them to be. Are your toes positive or negative?

Think for a moment about feelings as being neither good nor bad, not positive or negative. They're just sensations that happen inside you. Internal experiences. Annoying, wonderful, scary, confusing at times, but not harmful or wrong.

EVERY FEELING HAS VALUE

"He who has felt the deepest grief is best able to experience supreme happiness."

~ ALEXANDRE DUMAS

"The great object of life is sensation—to feel that we exist, even though in pain."

~ LORD BYRON

"Emotion is the chief source of all becoming-conscious. There can be no transforming of darkness into light and of apathy into movement without emotion."

~ CARL JUNG

"Living is an inherently emotional business."

~ DAVID BROOKS

"Frustration, despair, angst, anxiety, hurt, grief, unhappiness, envy, jealousy, and all the other painful emotions are catalysts of change in our lives. They motivate us to do things differently, to change our status quo."

~ KATE LEVINSON

"It is not the length of life, but the depth."

~ RALPH WALDO EMERSON

"Good manners have much to do with the emotions. To make them ring true, one must feel them, not merely exhibit them."

~ AMY VANDERBILT

"I keep telling you that feeling is not selective. You can't feel pain, you aren't gonna feel anything else either."

~ JUDITH GUEST

What makes us think of some feelings as negative is the fact that we don't particularly like them. We don't always enjoy being angry (although I sort of *do*), so we label anger a negative emotion, or even a "toxic" emotion—as if merely experiencing a feeling could corrode us from the inside!

Because we tend to confuse emotions with behavior (which I'll talk about a little later), anger is often confused with intentional behaviors like aggression and violence. But, like all feelings, pure anger is neither an intention nor a behavior. It's just a feeling, with no ability to harm.

We'll take another look at the problem of negativity in Chapter 7, "The Daunting Dozen: Top Twelve Wallowing Worries."

By the way, many "negative" feelings, including anxiety, sadness, and anger, can be caused or worsened by medical conditions. Blood sugar and hormone levels, lack of sleep, heart problems, and other physical conditions can directly affect your emotions. Have you had a checkup lately?

Once you know that your physical health is not directly causing your feelings, you can let go of any worry that there's something "negative" about your feelings.

Having Feelings in Public

Having (also known as witnessing, accepting, claiming, allowing, tolerating, or embracing) feelings happens when you're alive, awake, and aware of how you feel, but not acting on or talking about your feelings.

Think about the last time you were in a crowded public place. Did you know how every person around you was feeling at any given moment? Probably not.

Maybe someone right next to you was silently doing one of the following:

- Grieving a loss
- Feeling angry about an injustice
- Anxiously anticipating an event
- In despair over a breakup
- Glowing with pleasure, pride, or joy

Maybe you were having a feeling in public. Did you show it? Is it possible that others had no idea what you were feeling? Of course it is. We routinely hide how we feel in public. But it doesn't mean we're not secretly feeling something.

We're emotional beings; we feel things—even when

it's not convenient. Unless our emotions pile up and over-whelm our defenses, we can and do hide how we feel in certain situations (or for some of us, in most situations).

Please remember that when I talk about allowing yourself to have your feelings, I'm not even talking about showing them, let alone *doing* anything about them. I'm referring to the internal, private experience of feeling something. As if you were in a public place, feeling something.

There's a lot of room for feeling on the inside, without doing anything about it on the outside. Any and every emotion can be safely felt, without you or anyone else being harmed in the process.

Wallowing Means Never Having to Say You're Sorry

What images come to mind when you think of wallowing? Complaining nonstop to anyone who will listen? Drinking excessively without thinking about consequences? Calling people in tears...or refusing to answer the phone? These are behaviors. They're external, visible actions. They're activities someone else could point to and say, "She's complaining" or "He's drinking heavily" or "She's not answering the phone."

As you can see in Table 1 on page 55, wallowing is something quite different. Wallowing is an internal, private activity.

Wallowing is another name for consciously deciding

to have (i.e., witness, accept, allow, immerse yourself in, etc.) the emotions that are there inside you at the moment, without criticizing the emotions or yourself for having them.

Wallowing *constructively* means not only having your feelings, but being kind to yourself while you do it.

Table 1 compares and lists examples of three different ways of dealing with emotions—acting out, managing, and constructively wallowing in feelings. Most of us use some combination of these to deal with our emotions.

Table 1. Some Ways to Deal with Feelings

Outside (Public, visible)		Inside (Private, invisible)
Acting out feelings	Managing feelings	Constructive (w)allowing
Attacking others verbally or physically Driving too fast Eating or drinking too much Complaining constantly	Rehashing scenarios Obsessing Worrying Ignoring or suppressing feelings Trying to "let go" of feelings	Having, embracing, claiming, witnessing, accepting, allowing, and tolerating emotions Letting feelings be
Anxiety, alienation, emptiness, depression		Self-compassion, self-knowledge, renewed energy

The table distinguishes between what I'm calling external (acting out) and internal (managing, wallowing) ways of dealing with feelings. From left to right, the way we deal with emotions becomes more internal and leads away from unconscious acting out to greater awareness and, ultimately, emotional health.

As we saw in the Escalation Cycle described in Chapter 1, when we don't pay conscious attention to, and embrace, a feeling, we're in danger of acting it out. Feelings want our attention, and, when they don't get it, they get pushy. They start to express themselves through our behavior—in effect, controlling us. An unrealized need for emotional soothing, for example, might manifest as a big fat need to hit the jackpot at the casino, no matter how much of our savings it takes. Or an unacknowledged sense of rejection can translate into unintentionally catty behavior toward the person we think rejected us.

Once we become aware of unpleasant feelings— unmet needs, rejection, loneliness, regret, fear—we're less in danger of acting them out unconsciously. It's tempting to try to manage them through over-thinking, under-feeling, or both. We move out of the frying pan of unconsciously acting out our feelings, into the fire of our own feelings-management process. And managing feelings usually means *trying not to feel them*.

It's tiring to struggle against feeling the way we do. It doesn't lead to a good place. As indicated in Table 1, both acting out and managing feelings produce the same outcomes: anxiety, alienation, emptiness, and depression.

Constructive (w)allowing, like managing feelings, can't necessarily be observed from the outside.

You can wallow silently for five minutes without anyone knowing it, and feel a whole lot better for it. The trick is to wallow in feelings, rather than try to manage them.

Unlike managing feelings, wallowing doesn't involve a struggle of any kind. There you are, and there are your feelings, and all you have to do is allow what is, to be. Simple, right?

Even if the feelings are hard, it's easier to feel them than to pretend they're not there. Remember, wallowing just means feeling your feelings, whatever they are, and being nice to yourself while you do it. There's no hard work to do, no forcing yourself to do anything unnatural. Your feelings are coming up to be felt, so feel them. No need to perform the exhausting task of criticizing yourself, either. Just let it be.

Now that we're on the same page about emotions and feelings, the fact that there's no such thing as a negative emotion, what it means to just have a feeling, and how wallowing compares to other ways of coping, it's time to unravel a few more knots of potential misunderstanding.

Once we've busted all the myths that need busting, and you're ready for some healthy wallowing, you'll have the confidence you need to make it work for you.

Name That Feeling!

....

Unless you want your worst feelings to control your thoughts and behavior, you need to be able to experience and tolerate them.

This is made much easier if you can name your feelings. Too many of us didn't learn words for emotions when we were young (other than "@#&%*$!"). Sometimes, the only clues we got about feelings were when we were troubled by painful ones. And all we might have heard about them then was "Stop that," or something equally unconstructive.

Fortunately, emotional literacy—basically, knowing and naming feelings—is possible at any age. The six emotions with universally recognizable facial expressions are thought to be:

- anger
- joy
- sadness
- disgust
- fear
- surprise

But of course, there are other emotions and many, many other words to express feelings. The more you start noticing and naming feelings for yourself, the easier it becomes. Later in this chapter you'll practice naming feelings. First, let's make the important distinction between feelings and thoughts.

Feelings vs. Thoughts

It's impossible to deal effectively with feelings if you're not aware of them. That would be like trying to solve a problem you don't know you have.

If you're not familiar with your emotions, you're likely to end up thinking instead of feeling, using your head instead of your heart. So let's get acquainted with the difference between feelings and thoughts.

Just because we use the words "I feel" at the beginning of a sentence, doesn't mean we're describing an actual feeling. **Anything you describe using the words "I feel (that)," followed by a complete sentence, is not a feeling.**

For example, "I feel that you're being unfair" is not a feeling. In this case, "You're being unfair" is a complete sentence that represents a thought, not a feeling. We might as well change the statement to "I *think* you're being unfair."

Statements that start with "I feel *like*" often describe thoughts rather than feelings.

"I feel like a failure," for instance, is just another way of saying, "I feel that *I am a failure*," which conforms to the recipe for thoughts described above. Hence, "I feel like a failure" is not a feeling but a thought. ("I feel inadequate" might be a better way to capture the actual feeling in this case.)

The Substitution Test

If you can change the words "I feel" in a statement to

"I think" without changing any other words, and still be left with a meaningful sentence, you've described a thought and not a feeling.

Try this: "I feel it might be good to bring some extra forks on our picnic today." Is that a feeling?

Substitute "I think" for "I feel":

"I think it might be good to bring some extra forks on our picnic today."

The substitution of "I think" for "I feel" worked perfectly well; it makes sense without changing any other words in the sentence. This indicates that "I feel it might be good to bring some extra forks" expresses a thought and not a feeling.

When we say "I feel" followed by a full sentence like "he doesn't care if I live or die" instead of using a feeling word like "worthless" (as in, "I feel worthless"), we're pointing to something that triggers our feelings, not the feelings themselves.

Try the substitution test on the following:

I *feel* this situation is dangerous.

I *feel* that I should be compensated for this.

I *feel* you're being unreasonable.

Are these feelings or thoughts? Substitute "think" for "feel" without changing any other words and see if we get sentences that make sense:

I *think* this situation is dangerous.	✓	(Thought)
I *think* that I should be compensated for this.	✓	(Thought)
I *think* you're being unreasonable.	✓	(Thought)

Notice how each of these is something you can think about, but might or might not have actual feelings about. Thinking a situation is dangerous, for example, can be either just a passing thought, or a highly emotional experience—probably depending on whether you're *in* the situation.

Emotions aren't usually identified by complete sentences. They're generally described in a short word or phrase, like the ones in Table 2 on page 62.

To continue with the Substitution Test, let's return to "I feel" statements, and use actual feeling words.

Instead of saying "I feel this situation is dangerous," try using a feeling word. Let's try *scared*. The statement becomes, "I feel scared."

Let's make sure we're really describing a feeling with our new sentence, I feel scared, by using the Substitution Test. Try substituting "I think" for "I feel":

I think scared. ✗ (Feeling)

The substitution doesn't work, because "I think scared" is not a good sentence; you can't think a feeling any more than you can feel a thought.

Table 2. Some Feeling Words

Painful	<--->		Pleasant
Afraid	Inadequate	Accepted	Optimistic
Angry	Inferior	Amused	Peaceful
Anxious	Insecure	Appreciated	Pensive
Apathetic	Insignificant	Appreciative	Playful
Ashamed	Irritated	Aware	Pleased
Betrayed	Isolated	Calm	Powerful
Bewildered	Jealous	Cheerful	Present
Bored	Lonely	Cherished	Proud
Confused	Lost	Close	Respected
Defensive	Nervous	Confident	Respectful
Depressed	Off-balance	Connected	Sensuous
Despondent	Overwhelmed	Content	Stimulated
Disconnected	Regretful	Creative	Successful
Discouraged	Rejected	Daring	Surprised
Envious	Ridiculous	Elated	Thrilled
Embarrassed	Sad	Energetic	Trusting
Empty	Stuck	Engaged	Valuable
Frustrated	Stupid	Excited	Whole
Furious	Trapped	Fascinated	Worthwhile
Grieving	Unacceptable	Free	
Hateful	Unlovable	Grateful	
Helpless	Unsuccessful	Grounded	
Hopeless	Unwanted	Hopeful	
Hostile	Unworthy	Important	
Hurt	Wary	Included	
		Joyful	
		Loving	
		Nurtured	

If you *can't* successfully substitute "I think" for "I feel,"
you have a genuine feeling word.

Try it out:

I feel remorse → I think remorse   ✗ (Feeling)

I feel lonely → I think lonely   ✗ (Feeling)

I feel a sense of belonging → I   ✗ (Feeling)
   think a sense of belonging

Because the word "think" doesn't work in the above
examples, we know that "remorse," "lonely," and "a
sense of belonging" all describe feelings rather than
thoughts.

Exercise

1. Imagine what the people in the following scenarios
might feel. Fill in the blanks below using words provided
in Table 2, or some of your own. Just make sure you're
describing emotions, rather than thoughts.

A neighbor asks Felix to feed her goldfish while
she's away. Felix agrees, but forgets to do it, and the fish
dies. How might Felix feel?

Examples: Sad, remorseful, annoyed...etc.

_____

Felicia has some ideas for her club's fund-raising
efforts. She mentions them to the club president, who
promptly puts Felicia's ideas on the agenda for discussion at the next meeting. How might Felicia feel?

_____

Fred's best friend's girlfriend makes a pass at him. How might Fred feel?

_____

Frieda runs out of gas on the freeway and ends up parked on the shoulder. A stranger in a pickup truck stops and puts a gallon of gasoline in her tank. How might Frieda feel?

_____

2. Each of the sentences below incorrectly uses the words "I feel" even though it describes a thought. Correct each sentence by filling in the blank with a feeling word.

There are no right or wrong answers here. Different people feel different feelings in the same situations. The point of this exercise is to get you used to describing emotions instead of thoughts.

Example: "I feel that I should have been promoted." → *I feel <u>frustrated</u>.*

"I feel that I behaved badly." →
    I feel _____.

"I feel this is a good time to try something new." →
    I feel _____.

"I feel that he isn't respecting my wishes." →
    I feel _____.

"I feel that I did a good job." →
    I feel _____.

"I feel that a vacation might be a good idea." →
    I feel _____.

What are some feelings you've experienced recently?

_____

How do you feel right this minute? _____

_____

Feelings vs. Behavior

....

Now that we've made the distinction between feelings and thoughts, there's another crucial difference to note. It's the separation between feelings and behavior (also known as actions). To feel good about embracing our emotions, we need to know that it's a safe thing to do. What makes feelings safe is that *we don't have to act them out in order to experience them.*

Being angry, for example, is not the same as shouting, cursing, or getting physical. These last three are behaviors, or actions, as opposed to feelings. They're pretty good signs that someone is angry. But they're not the same as anger. It's perfectly possible to be extremely angry and yet not break anything, hurt anyone, or turn Facebook into a weapon.

Feeling sad, desperate, or hopeless is not the same as killing yourself. Millions of people experience these emotions every day without taking action to end their lives; emotions do not inevitably lead to action... Thank goodness.

Because most of us didn't learn as children how to deal constructively with difficult emotions, we worry that just allowing ourselves to experience a feeling means we will—or should—act it out, with negative consequences. And this belief is reinforced by the news media. We regularly hear about real people acting on feelings of rage, hatred, fear, or despair and ending up dead or in prison. No wonder we're scared of our own emotions!

But most of us don't act on our feelings all the time. From the workplace to a wedding, anywhere there are clear expectations for behavior, we generally manage to contain whatever feelings we might have, especially if they don't match up with how we're supposed to act.

We all have the skills to feel one way and act another. Have you ever received an unattractive, unwanted, or bizarre gift from a well-meaning friend and pretended to be gleeful about it? We know very well what it's like to hide our true feelings. And appropriately so, since we're social beings. We do need to be able to manage our *behavior*.

Notice I said behavior, not feelings. Since we're capable of acting differently from how we feel, we don't need to try to keep a stranglehold on "negative" emotions. We can stop hiding our feelings from ourselves.

Most of us are uncomfortable with the idea of having our thoughts controlled and censored by the "Thought Police." So why do we put up with the "Emotion Police" in our own heads? Don't be your own oppressor. Let yourself—and your feelings—be.

Allowing yourself to experience emotions without judgment or fear is at the center of constructive wallowing, and it's one of the most liberating things you can do for yourself. Don't confuse feeling bad with acting bad; feeling is something you can safely do without negative social consequences.

Also, don't confuse strong emotions with being out of control. Becoming more accepting of your feelings will make you feel more in control of yourself, not less. It's counterintuitive, but I've found it to be true, and so have many of my clients.

Elio Frattaroli,[1] in his excellent book *Healing the Soul in the Age of the Brain,* put it this way:

"I have found that most people...are skeptical of the idea that simply by feeling an uncomfortable feeling they can develop more of a sense of control over it. [But] in fact...we tend to be at our most controlling when we feel least in control, not when we feel strong but when we feel weak. We try to control things primarily because we are afraid of them."

Once you know that feelings aren't dangerous, you can relax and let them be. There's no need to control them if you don't find them quite so scary.

Control your behavior, by all means. But, as Frattaroli goes on to say, "it is an illusion to believe we are ever truly in control of our inner processes." Save your energy; let your feelings be what they are.

Good People Have Bad Feelings Too

Feelings are not values. If you feel indignant about something, it's not because you're an indignant person. You're just indignant about this particular thing. Accept it. Don't make a big moral dilemma out of having an unpleasant feeling. I know: You want to feel like a good person. So do I. But what makes us good people is our choices. And feelings are not by choice.

We'll talk more about this issue throughout the book. I want you to know that you can relax and let yourself off the hook if you feel annoyed, irritated, resentful, envious, etc., etc., etc. You're not a bad person just because you have the kinds of emotions that usually underlie bad behavior. We're all subject to the same emotions—good, bad, and in between. It has nothing to do with our moral character.

Remember, feelings are like your toes. How much does your goodness depend on your toes? The correct answer is to laugh at the absurdity of letting your toes— or your feelings—reflect on whether you're good.

Judge yourself by your actions, by all means, because they can be good or bad, moral or immoral. Actions almost always involve making choices. Feelings never do.

If you're not convinced yet, don't worry. I'll try again later.

How Hurting Heals

In the previous chapters I've referred to the relationship between (w)allowing in feelings and becoming whole, and I think that connection is worth expanding on.

You may recall from Chapter 1 that when we don't allow ourselves to feel the way we do, we move away from wholeness. We become divided against ourselves, and we end up feeling half empty. And without our emotions, that's exactly what we are.

If you've been trying to not-have certain emotions (even though, let's be honest, you do have them), you've had to do some serious mental gymnastics in order *not* to feel how you feel. You have to wall off the parts of yourself that feel that way.

You end up pushing a part of yourself away in order to keep from feeling bad. This leads to a sense of being all in pieces inside, or just empty, or both, which makes you feel bad anyway.

It's strange that when someone gets really sad and starts crying about something, we say they "went to pieces." That seems backwards. Crying means we're connected with our pain, rather than cut off from it. When we cry, we're whole in the sense that we're connected with ourselves, including the part of us that hurts.

When we try to be tough, try to ignore our pain, try not to cry, that's when we're suddenly in at least two pieces: One piece is in pain and the other piece wants to be strong by denying the pain.

Contrary to popular opinion, the people who look like they're holding it together are often the ones who've fallen apart.

The Life Cycle of a Feeling

Some years ago I visited my parents, who were still living in my childhood home, for a family reunion. My mom had bought a bunch of flowers for the living room, and my brother pointed out a unique stem bearing "Siamese twin" blossoms. We marveled together at the sideways figure eight, the symbol for infinity, at the center of this unusual flower.

The bouquet's strong aroma and brilliant colors seemed to celebrate our reunion like a trumpet flourish, and the infinity-shaped bloom seemed to me a testament to the wonder of Life itself.

Our visit was filled with the sweetness of nostalgia and belonging. I slept soundly when visiting my family, as if some part of me knew that I was "home" and could relax with my loved ones safe and sound nearby.

Several days into the visit, I found myself surprised that the lively bouquet, including the special double-centered blossom, had begun to fade and droop. I'd foolishly forgotten that time didn't stand still just because I was home again. Suddenly, I was sad. The withering of the "infinity" flower, previously so full of life and promise, was an unwelcome reminder that nothing lasts forever.

Until that moment, I'd allowed myself the fantasy that my family and my childhood home would always be there, untouched by the passage of time. I had cocooned myself inside an impossible dream of always being able to go home again.

My father died just a few years later and my mom

moved to a smaller home. I often think back to that bittersweet moment of truth that foreshadowed the end of Home.

Feelings are like flowers. They grow, then bloom, then wither and die. This process of taking root, thriving, and then dying is Nature's plan for feelings, just as it is for flowers and all living things.

Each of our feelings is supposed to take root, grow, bloom, and then wither, eventually disappearing altogether—until the next one comes along. No particular feeling is designed to last forever, any more than any particular flower is. A flower *garden* can last a lifetime, but each particular flower has a natural cycle, at the end of which it's done and gone.

You can see the feeling cycle at work in very young children. They haven't been around long enough to develop a backlog of unexpressed emotions, nor have they perfected the suppression of feelings yet. Each feeling, as it comes up, is fully felt and usually expressed in behavior as well.

A healthy child doesn't brood, isn't depressed, and doesn't get stuck in one emotional gear. Healthy children are all over the map emotionally. And because they're not yet in control of their behavior, they also spontaneously express their emotions in ways we as adults wouldn't necessarily do. I'm not suggesting we act like young children. But let's not throw out the baby with the bathwater.

Healthy children don't have sticky feelings. A toddler who is apparently in heart-wrenching despair can be sleeping peacefully five minutes later and wake up full of joy and play, the despair completely forgotten. The younger the child, the more Nature—and less learned behavior—is at play.

Even before it's fully mature, the human brain develops the ability to interfere with the body's natural processes, and to corrupt them.

For example, if we throw up our food to avoid gaining weight, we interrupt the natural process of digestion.

When we pick at a scab, we interfere with the body's natural process for healing wounds.

And when we try to ignore our emotions instead of experiencing them, we interfere with the natural process that allows feelings to dissipate.

But Nature is bossy!

Your stomach will try to digest any non-toxic thing that goes into it. Your skin will do its best to repair an open wound. And your heart will keep trying to let your unfelt feelings complete their natural cycle, by continually bringing those feelings to your attention.

Trying to "let go" of existing feelings, therefore, creates more problems than it solves. It interferes not only with personal wholeness, but with Nature itself.

"Anger issues" and "shame spirals" are fairly common, but you can travel thousands of miles without bumping into someone who has "happiness issues" or complains of being in a "contentment spiral." The positive emotions feel good, so we leave them alone. In other words, we *let them go*. And what happens? They do go, and always sooner than we'd like.

Have you ever wondered why we usually don't have much trouble "letting go of" (i.e., [w]allowing in) joy, contentment, love, or ecstasy? These so-called positive feelings cause most of us far less trouble than the so-called negative ones—anger, fear, despair, shame, etc. Obviously, they feel good. They're also socially acceptable.

We enjoy it when positive emotions take root, grow, and blossom within us. We don't bother to interfere with this process. We want those feelings to thrive. We think we would love it if they stayed in bloom forever. And so we just witness, enjoy, and embrace them as long as we can.

We really let those positive feelings go. When they're through with us and they leave us, we kiss them goodbye with a sigh, and look forward to their next visit. Good feelings don't last forever *because* we successfully let them go.

Pleasant emotions follow Nature's plan without interference, and so after they grow and blossom, they wither and die, just as all feelings are meant to do. Ironically, it's our whole-hearted acceptance—our having, embracing, witnessing, and tolerating—of them that allows these feelings to move through us, and eventually to die a natural death.

It's easy to let the good feelings go in this way. But how do we do that with the bad ones?

How to Let Painful Feelings Go

It's common to believe that if you have yucky feelings about something, and you can't *do* anything about it, you should just "let it go." You're supposed to somehow let go of your fear, your regret, your longing, your grief. Whatever the painful feeling is, according to popular wisdom, you must simply "let it go."

If you're like me, you might have scratched your head and said, "Well, okay…. But how do I *do* that?"

You're absolutely right to question how you're supposed to make that happen. You're one hundred percent correct in NOT understanding how to do that, because the way we were taught to let go of feelings doesn't make sense. And it doesn't work.

The way we're told to let go of feelings amounts to ignoring them. We try to ignore bad feelings. But it doesn't make them go away. It has the opposite effect, triggering the escalation cycle (see Chapter 1) and making them hang around longer than necessary.

In an effort to let go of painful feelings, most of us end up stuffing our feelings down somewhere inside ourselves, effectively putting them in a cage, locking the door and trying to forget where the key is. Which, of course, is exactly the opposite of letting them go.

If you have wild rabbits living in your yard, and someone tells you to let them go, do you round them up and put them in a cage? Of course not. That wouldn't be letting them go, it would be hanging on to them.

Stuffing feelings down is like putting rabbits in a

cage; it makes it impossible for them to go anywhere, let alone "away."

And once those bunnies are locked up together, you shouldn't be surprised if they (and probably a good many more) are still there the next time you look. The only way out is through the door...that you locked. Expecting them to somehow leave anyway doesn't make sense.

Feelings want to be let go, but they need to go on Nature's terms. They have to exit through our hearts, where we can feel them. They want to grow and bloom there before they die. Rabbits want to do what rabbits do; feelings want to take root and live out their short lives in our hearts. That's their nature, and it's our design, too.

You probably don't want a field full of ugly feelings blooming in your heart. Maybe you'd rather not feel those bad ones at all. But in order to let go of painful emotions, you have to feel the pain, and let it matter to you. And that's what makes it so hard. Wallowing is an act of courage as well as compassion.

You know that saying that's popular at the gym, "No pain, no gain"? It's certainly true if you want to let your more difficult feelings go for good.

If you're in emotional pain, you're going to be hurting whether you embrace that pain or push it away. It's far more constructive to embrace it, have it, feel it and let it "go" through its paces. Since you're going to be hurt whether you embrace that pain or not, wouldn't you rather be there for yourself and make it the most productive, healing experience possible?

Two words: Feel it. Just feel your pain. Let it go where it wants to go with you.

On the other side of the pain, you'll have something to show for your courage. In addition to reclaiming lost parts of yourself, you'll gain confidence through facing the challenge and living through it. You'll know more about yourself because your feelings will remind you who you are and what matters to you. You'll feel better about yourself because you trusted yourself to be there for you, and you came through.

Any emotions you have right this second are there whether you want them to be or not. The ones that will be in your heart tomorrow will be there whether you want them there or not. Your only two choices are to accept that fact or to struggle against it.

Do you accept that gravity pulls objects to the ground?

Do you accept that you breathe air instead of water?

Do you accept the fact that with age come wrinkles?

Wait. Forget the third one. The point is, feelings are a fact of life, just like gravity and biology. If you jump from a high place, you'll fall to the ground. If you're poked with something sharp, you'll bleed. And if something happens in your life, you'll have feelings about it.

You can't beat Mother Nature. The smartest choice you can make is to understand and work with her.

You Can't Choose Your Feelings

Unlike the old-school, pull-yourself-up-by-your-boot-straps approach to dealing with hardships large and small, I'm suggesting that you work with, rather than against, Nature's plan for feelings. When you go with the natural flow, your emotional life will be varied instead of monotone, dynamic instead of chronic, colorful instead of gray.

Allowing feelings to be what they are is efficient and effective in a way that suppressing them simply is not. It leads to relief and doesn't interfere with emotional health. Actually, it promotes it.

Perhaps the most important reason to (w)allow in your emotions is to learn by experience that just having feelings can't hurt you, and that emotions don't have to control your thoughts or behavior.

It's more often our unacknowledged or unnamed feelings that control us than the ones we're aware of. What we don't acknowledge imprisons us, according to David Viscott, M.D.[2], author of *Emotional Resilience: Simple Truths for Dealing with the Unfinished Business of Your Past.*

To return to the absurd idea that you can get rid of a yucky feeling just by "letting it go," think about what it means to let go of your body temperature. That's as impossible as it is meaningless. Your body temperature exists, and it is what it is, and that's all there is to it.

Your temperature may change. It might be higher or lower today than tomorrow. Same with feelings; they hover around whatever's normal for you in your life right now, and they change according to circumstances.

The last time I checked, the part of the brain that controls your body temperature was the hypothalamus, which is physically and functionally separate from the prefrontal cortex, where decision-making occurs. That's why your temperature isn't under your conscious control.

The limbic system, which is the part of your brain where emotions are born, is also separate from the prefrontal cortex, and there is zero evidence that the latter can reliably control the former.

Repeat after me: "I can't choose my feelings." I know you've been led to believe that you can, but you can't. If you could, you wouldn't be reading this book, or any self-help book. You'd simply choose to be happy and that would be that.

Remember the other little tidbit that follows from what we've just said. *Since you can't choose your feelings, you can't be bad for having them.*

Did you ever hear the following when you were small: "Stop crying, or I'll give you something to cry about"? If you heard this often, you must have thought you had the power to choose your emotions. Otherwise, why would anyone tell you to stop feeling? Surely they wouldn't tell you to do something that was impossible.

In order to decide not to cry, you have to try not to be sad. It's heartbreaking how many children attempt this impossible feat every single day. They learn to ignore their own feelings, to stuff them and pretend they don't have them...until they forget they're pretending.

If you were one of those children, you don't have to try anymore to control the uncontrollable. You can choose to let yourself have the feelings you have. Without guilt. Without shame. And without anyone getting hurt or your being a bad person.

Summary

- Emotions are neither negative nor positive.
- Having feelings is different from acting on them.
- Managing feelings often means trying to ignore them.
- Feelings are not the same as thoughts.
- Feelings are separate from behavior.
- Feelings are neither moral nor immoral; don't be your own "Emotion Police."
- Feelings have a life cycle.
- We can't choose our feelings.

PART II

Dive In

Chapter 4

11 Good Reasons to Wallow

S o far we've discussed how emotions need to be felt in order to go away, and I hope I've convinced you that it's safe and healthy to feel them. In this part of the book we'll look at a specific tool—the T-R-U-T-H Technique—for wallowing constructively. I'll introduce you to several people who are using the Technique to deal with some very painful feelings. Of course, you'll also get a chance to take it for a spin yourself.

Wallowing constructively is hard, so you'll need some motivation to stick with it. Here are some specific reasons to get good at this process and make it a life-long habit.

Reason #1: You have no choice

I'm sorry to be the one to tell you this, but you're going to experience painful feelings whether you embrace them or not, off and on for the rest of your life. There's no magic thought that will protect you from unhappiness. No way to attract constant joy. No mantra to ward off negativity once and for all. But this is GREAT news because, if you accept this reality, you're free at last! You don't have to struggle to be something you're not; you can just be yourself. You can use your energy in more productive ways than fighting with your emotions. This self-acceptance will make you more powerful, and even allow you to become more joyful, than you've ever been when you were trying so hard to be happy.

There is relief available when you feel down, and it comes from making the choice to embrace reality. It may not sound like a lot of fun, but the rewards are substantial. When you embrace your true feelings, unpleasant as they may be, you gain integrity and access to the vastly underrated joys of authenticity.

Embracing a negative feeling doesn't mean giving up. Remember that feelings are separate from behavior. You can experience your emotions consciously and still decide to do something that goes completely against them. A good example is when you're about to give a speech and you feel like ripping off your tie or your high heels and sprinting out of there instead because you're so nervous. But, rather than obeying anxiety's commands, you proceed to the podium and give the best speech you can.

We've already seen that you don't get to choose whether to have painful feelings. If you don't like giving speeches and you have to give them anyway, you're going to have feelings about that. Your only choice is whether to acknowledge your emotional state or use up your energy struggling against it, adding misery to pain.

Wallowing doesn't make feelings bigger, and ignoring feelings doesn't make them smaller. On the contrary, it's ignoring feelings that makes them bigger because they get stuck instead of moving on, and add their force to new feelings of the same type.

So since you're going to have yucky feelings along the way, you might as well learn how to acknowledge them, let them matter to you, and allow them to move freely through you on their way to oblivion. This will have the added benefit of increasing your energy, your integrity, and your self-esteem.

Reason #2:
It may be good for your health

It's generally understood that chronic stress is bad for health. And when you repeatedly try to control what can't be controlled (your emotions), you're cooking up a batch of exactly that: chronic stress.

The National Institute of Mental Health defines

stress as the brain's response to any demand. Imagine the constant demand on your brain when negative emotions have to be corralled and quarantined. Bad feelings that are new have to be suppressed as they're triggered, and old ones still hanging around have to be managed to keep them from resurfacing.

The tighter a rein you keep on your feelings, the more likely you are to suffer the effects of chronic stress. These include lowered function of your immune, digestive, and reproductive systems. Think more colds and allergies, upset stomach, and low libido. Not a pretty picture.

(W)allowing in the feelings you have is a healthy way to let go of stress by going with the flow. As the Borg said on *Star Trek* and as we saw in Reason #1 above: "Resistance is futile." If you can't beat 'em, you might as well roll with 'em.

I find that refusing to do battle with my painful feelings lets me be more relaxed about the fact that I have them. I'm not trying to control the uncontrollable, and that's a huge stress-reducer. Clients tell me they feel less uptight and anxious when they acknowledge and allow themselves to have their difficult feelings.

If you're used to ignoring bad feelings, or trying to find the silver lining in every dark cloud, it might feel scary to let them roll over you. But, if you consider that your health may be at stake, you might find some motivation to get good at going with the flow.

Reason #3: Get your energy back

I've got a friend who's been working hard for years to find her voice in relationships. As a child, she would have been physically assaulted by her father if she had spoken out against him, even to defend herself. Because of the threat of physical violence, speaking up for herself quickly became traumatic for her. Nevertheless, she's taken it upon herself as an adult to face what feels like grave danger in learning to speak up for herself in her relationships. This includes letting family members know they've disappointed her.

At this point she's able to initiate conversations that almost anyone would find difficult, with people who are important to her. However, it takes a ton of energy for her to do this, and most of it is spent managing her own fear about what she's doing.

That she's able to overcome her fear and start a difficult conversation at all is a testament to her courage and her will to grow. There's still a part of her that's convinced the other person is going to fly into a rage and start swinging at her if they don't like what she's saying. Imagine yourself in her shoes; would you be able to do it? I'm not sure I would.

Since so much of my friend's energy is being utilized to manage her anxiety during these conversations, and her focus is on saying what she needs to say despite her terror of consequences, it's no wonder she has few resources left to notice how her words are affecting the person she's talking to. Sometimes this leads to hard feelings on the other side, but she's managed to make repairs as needed and her relationships are evolving in the direction of greater intimacy. She is finding her voice. My friend's story is a triumph of the human will to overcome early trauma, and it also demonstrates the zero-sum nature of emotional energy.

During what feels like a dangerous situation, whatever energy is directed toward managing fear is necessarily diverted from other tasks. If the situation isn't perceived as that dangerous, the energy that would have been used to control the impulse to flee might be used instead for diplomacy tasks like modulating the pacing or the tone of voice, or reading nonverbal cues from the listener and modifying the message as needed to communicate effectively.

Similarly, it takes energy to suppress or distract ourselves from our own emotions. Because we don't have unlimited energy, it has to be stolen from other tasks. It does take energy to do those mental gymnastics I mentioned in Chapter 3, and that taps our reserves. The longer we struggle against our own feelings, the more depleted we become.

When we allow our feelings to flow through us, instead of managing them or acting them out with our behavior, we regain all the energy we were previously using to fight them. This energy can be redirected to the physical or mental things we need or want to do.

Reason #4:
If you can't feel bad, you won't feel good

My college boyfriend loved camping in the wilderness, so we went camping many times. That was how this city girl figured out she prefers the city! I didn't appreciate long hikes through bear-filled forests with a heavy pack on my back, but that wasn't the worst of it. I had a hard time with sleeping on the ground, being cold all night, and having to get up in pitch darkness and drop my drawers to pee somewhere outside the tent, hopefully not on our supplies, before getting back into "bed" to shiver for a few more hours, waiting for dawn and sunlight.

And yet...twenty-five years later, what I remember most about those camping trips was how good the food tasted. Macaroni and cheese from a box cooked over an open fire after a day of trekking over rough terrain is nothing like the macaroni and cheese from a box you might make in the kitchen at home. It's ambrosia. Nothing you've ever eaten while sitting comfortably at the dinner table ever tasted so divine.

Hardship enhances pleasure. The harder it is to build a good fire, the more we enjoy it once it gets going. The longer we hike, the better it feels to rest. The more heated the argument over whether to spend the next weekend camping, the better it feels to make up. You get the idea.

Opposites define each other. If we never had bad days, how would we know to appreciate the good ones? Trying to deny what's unpleasant and acknowledge only the good in life is a mistake. If the only facts and feelings we notice are good ones, then good things become just the way things are instead of something to savor or celebrate.

IF YOU'RE NOT WALLOWING, YOU'RE NOT LIVING

"I have known the joy and pain of friendship. I have served and been served. I have made some good enemies for which I am not a bit sorry. I have loved unselfishly, and I have fondled hatred with the red-hot tongs of Hell. That's living."

~ ZORA NEALE HURSTON

"I think the highest and lowest points are the important ones. Anything else is just...in between."

~ JIM MORRISON

"If you've never eaten while crying you don't know what life tastes like."

~ JOHANN WOLFGANG VON GOETHE

"Life is something that happens when you can't get to sleep."

~ FRAN LEBOWITZ

"Life is not a problem to be solved, but a reality to be experienced."

~ SØREN KIERKEGAARD

"Live to the point of tears."

~ ALBERT CAMUS

"Those who truly live life to the fullest will bear the full cup of suffering. Only those who are willing to pay the price in pain and anguish find life full to the brim."

~ ROBERT DYKSTRA

Also, because of how feelings work, it's just not possible to suppress the unpleasant ones without suppressing all of them. Anyone who takes an anti-depressant that works will tell you it's also an "anti-thrillant." There's a bit of all-or-nothing about the way feelings operate.

Imagine there's a barn full of butterflies, of all colors, and you want to let out just the yellow ones. The only way to free them is to open a window or a door. But when you do that, all sorts of butterflies can get out, not just the yellow ones.

Feelings are like butterflies in a barn; when a window is open, they can all get out. When the doors and windows are closed, they're all stuck inside. We act as if we can enjoy our positive feelings and ignore our more troubling ones, but we really can't. Think about it: If we were capable of trapping and subduing only our yucky feelings, and letting the good ones flow through us, we would be happy most of the time, wouldn't we? Nobody would be in therapy, no one would ever cry or get angry; we'd simply suppress the troublesome feelings like regret and worry and sadness—leaving them in the barn, as it were—and we'd engage in contentment and peace and joy instead.

The result of letting negative emotions flow by wallowing in them is that positive emotions are experienced more deeply as well. When you were trying not to feel despair, it wasn't safe to feel deep joy; the lines are too blurry, and you might have accidentally opened the door to sorrow.

Pleasant and unpleasant emotions are like up and

down, yin and yang, light and dark; you can't have one without the other. How could you enjoy the good without knowing what bad feels like? Your quality of life is measured in emotions. Every pleasure in life is, at its root, an emotional pleasure. The very feeling of being alive is an emotional experience. Constructive wallowing, which allows us to open the doors and windows and experience *all* our emotions more fully, is therefore necessary for a joyful life.

Reason #5: You're never more alone than when you abandon yourself

If you feel lonely frequently, could it be that you're lonely for yourself? When we don't (w)allow in our emotions, they get quarantined, along with the parts of ourselves they're attached to, out of our reach. The more we store our emotions away, the more of ourselves we're cut off from. This leaves us feeling in pieces instead of whole.

To be truly happy, we need to reunite with our hurt selves. When we're in pain, we need someone to care. We need to be able to say to ourselves, "I see that you're hurting, and I'm so very sorry." If we can't or won't accept from ourselves that compassionate attention, how can we accept it from anyone else?

By wallowing in your wounded feelings instead of pushing them aside, you provide yourself with caring company. You send yourself a message of love and concern. You feel like someone is really there for you, asserting your goodness. Stuffing or suppressing your feelings, on the other hand, sends a message of "I don't want to hear it," leaving you alone with your pain.

If you think back to an earlier time in your life, you might discover that you were left alone like this. Maybe not physically, but emotionally. If this happened often, it's probably how you learned to abandon yourself. People whose emotions were given sufficient positive attention by important others when they were young don't usually suffer from chronic loneliness, nor do they tend to abandon themselves when they feel bad. They have a healthy curiosity and concern about their own feelings. They try to nurture themselves when they feel blue if there's no one else around to do that for them.

But for those of us who didn't get the memo that said, "Your feelings matter," it's likely that we'll repeat the pattern of abandoning ourselves in our hours of need. We just never learned anything different.

Wallowing in our true feelings constructively reconnects us with who we are, provides a blueprint for self-nurturing, and soothes loneliness as nothing else can.

Reason #6:
What we don't acknowledge, controls us

"I always end up with men who cheat on me."

"I seem to be a magnet for clients from hell."

"My friendships just peter out after a certain period of time."

Do you see patterns in your life? If you do, you might be on to something. We don't end up in the same kinds of situations time after time after time just by happenstance. The odds are against that level of coincidence. When you spot a pattern in your relationships, your career, or both, you can assume there are unconscious beliefs at work. They may be the opposite of what you consciously think or want to believe, and yet they're pulling you toward those very situations that are as familiar as they are frustrating, annoying, or depressing.

For example, if you have an unconscious expectation of being cheated on by a partner, it will seem normal to you when your partner cheats, even though it's painful. That hidden expectation will cause you to ignore the red flags that are almost always there right from the get-go with cheaters, and you'll be blind-sided when it happens again.

In order to change a pattern like this, you need to explore the unconscious expectation that it will happen. As crazy as the question may seem, you need to ask, "What might be good about someone cheating on me?" A way of getting at the answer to that is to ask yourself, "What would happen if I found someone who *didn't* cheat on me? What would be required of me in a genuinely committed relationship? What would I have to face in myself if I weren't disappointed in my partner?"

Unacknowledged feelings, like unconscious beliefs, can also create unwanted experiences. They work in a similar way—that is, calling the shots from behind the scenes, in the shadows outside your awareness. Any emotions you've repeatedly suppressed in the past are inside you right this minute, ready to add their force to any similar feelings triggered in the present and future.

If you tend to overreact or feel especially sensitive to specific situations (i.e., if you have familiar buttons that often get pushed), your reaction is likely a signpost pointing to feelings from the past that haven't been thoroughly addressed.

To transform overreaction and/or high sensitivity to certain situations or people, we have to revisit and feel the original feelings that created our sensitivity, and give them the compassion, respect, and caring they're due. We need to understand and integrate them into our life stories. Only this will break their hold over us. Eventually we'll be able to respond differently when those same buttons get pushed.

Constructive wallowing not only helps to deal with new feelings that threaten to control us, it can also provide a way out of seemingly permanent patterns that make us feel out of control. See more on this subject in Chapter 9's Q and A.

Note: If you suspect you have trauma from an incident or incidents in the past, please find a mental health professional to work with. Long-standing trauma exerts control over us, and it doesn't tend to resolve itself without intervention beyond self-help.

Reason #7: You'll feel better sooner

Two-year-old twins Mike and Ignatius go to the hair salon with Mom for their very first haircut. Both are afraid of getting up in the chair near the scary scissors, and both try to bolt when their stylists are ready for them.

Mom catches Mike by the shirt, but Ignatius makes it out the door and halfway down the sidewalk in a jiffy. While the stylist helps Mike into the chair and assures him it won't hurt, Mom goes after Ignatius.

Mike gives in and sits in the chair, resigned to his fate. He cries because he's frightened, but he knows he can't go home until his hair is trimmed. He toughs it out while Mom tries to manage the fit that Ignatius is now throwing in the waiting area. Ten minutes later, Mike has a lollipop and a handsome new 'do. He's relieved and proud to have survived the ordeal. It seems like magic that the scissors didn't hurt his hair!

Meanwhile, Ignatius is busy struggling against the inevitable. He eyes his brother's lollipop. He wants one too, but doesn't want to earn it by getting in the chair. The nice stylist promises him a lollipop after his haircut, but he just wants to go home. Mom picks him up while he struggles, screaming, and she and the stylist attempt to put him in the chair. He slides out, kicking with his entire body. He will not have his hair cut! Even after they manage to maneuver Ignatius into the chair, he thrashes his head back and forth, making it unsafe for the stylist to get close with the scissors.

By the time Mom and the stylist have almost

exhausted Ignatius, he has thoroughly exhausted them. Mom gives up and takes his hand, leading him away. Victory is his!

"We'll have to try again tomorrow," says Mom. "No lollipop today, because you didn't get your hair cut."

"Noooooo!" screams Ignatius. He thought the ordeal would end if he could hold out long enough. Now, in addition to having screamed himself hoarse and having no lollipop, he's going to have to face the same situation tomorrow. This was not a victory after all.

In the car on the way home, Mike sleeps peacefully. His haircut was scary at first, but once he gave into it, he found that it wasn't as bad as he'd feared.

When we feel bad, we want to feel better as soon as possible. Like Ignatius, we want to get out of here and go home! We want to feel good again without going through the crucible of feeling bad. Nature gives us motivation to do things that feel good and to stay away from things that feel bad, so we can avoid pain and seek pleasure. It's perfectly natural to shy away from an unpleasant experience. Unfortunately, once we have emotional pain, it's too late to avoid it. Try as we might, we can't not-feel bad when we already feel bad. Mike knew that, once he was in the chair, it was pointless to resist getting a haircut. But we don't all share Mike's wisdom and fortitude.

The fastest way out of emotional pain is by going through it, i.e., by feeling it and tolerating it until it passes. Trying not to feel the way we do only prolongs our bad feelings, gives power to them, and cements our misery in place. Like Ignatius, we can struggle against our pain today, but doing so will only invite continued struggle tomorrow.

When you (w)allow in your true feelings, they will run their natural course. Once they've done their thing, they'll go away on their own.

Don't confuse wallowing with curing a feeling. Some feelings are like Barney, the cheerful purple dinosaur: They're big and they have lots of friends. Each instance of a feeling needs your full embrace. You may need to feel the same way a dozen times or more about a specific subject before you're through having strong feelings about it, but that doesn't mean you're not getting anywhere. If you embrace the emotion fully each time, you can rest assured that you're whittling away at the backlog.

Reason #8: It's natural

There's nothing weird or wrong about wallowing. In nature, animals wallow in mud to coat their skin and protect them from insect bites. Okay, okay. You're not an animal, and you have a reliable spray that keeps insects at bay. But the kind of wallowing we're discussing, while it would never appear as the subject of a nature program like a warthog wallowing in mud, is still natural for human beings.

All over the world, and throughout history, humans have created socially acceptable ways to wallow in diffi-cult feelings. There's an implicit understanding that it's

Nature's way to slow down and embrace emotional pain when it threatens to overwhelm us. Just as animals lie low when they're sick or grieving (I've seen dogs and cats grieve, and I'll bet other animals do, too), we do the same in hard times.

For instance, the loss of a loved one—or even a leader or other public figure—is often marked by particular forms of dress and behavior. Wearing black clothes, or a special ribbon or armband, signifies to everyone that the wearer is in mourning. By this others know they should cut the mourner some slack. Avoiding parties, which a bereaved person might naturally want to do, is accepted and even encouraged for a time following a loss.

National holidays tend to commemorate emotional events and well-loved people who inspire emotion in others. It's no coincidence that there's a national holiday celebrating the life and work of Dr. Martin Luther King, Jr., but no national holiday celebrating potatoes, even though potatoes are very popular. We pause as a nation in order to make room for emotion.

National days off, and days we take off personally following difficult passages in life, invite us to take stock of what's meaningful to us and to experience ourselves as emotional beings. It's part of the rhythm of life; sometimes we're moving forward and being productive, and other times we're pausing and letting the past catch up with us.

All feelings deserve our attention, and it's good to reflect on the depth and breadth of understanding across cultures that it's natural, at least to some degree, to (w)allow in emotion from time to time.

Reason #9:
We all have something that needs healing

You may not even realize it, but the reason for today's low mood or irritation could be as simple, and as profound, as a need for healing. You may still need to heal from yesterday's hurts. Maybe you didn't have time to feel the pain before, and now it's tapping you on the shoulder, asking, "Do you have time for me now?"

It's too easy to think of our feelings as inconsequential and therefore ignore them when they arise. We mainly focus on what we need to *do*, especially in challenging situations. Our feelings just seem to get in the way when the fur is flying. We believe what we really need to do is to take care of business by deciding on the proper course of action. Of course, that's a good thing to do, but it's also how we get caught up in the vicious circle of an emotional backlog.

Once the feelings come up, you can refuse to wallow by ignoring or suppressing or trying to change them. And you may be successful in the short term. But in the long term, it's a losing strategy that does more harm than good.

If you don't acknowledge and feel your feelings, they don't heal, and therefore they don't resolve. You're stuck with them. Forever! There's no release, and the clumps of stuck feelings leave you with less room for happiness.

Ignored emotions stay mostly out of your awareness, along with parts of you that you will miss. Or they dance around the edges of your mind, bothering you at inconvenient times, making you feel like a bad person and sucking the joy from your years.

Wallowing is an ongoing exercise regimen that builds your "feeling muscles" so that you can perform the rewarding work of healing yourself, and building nurturing relationships with others. Wallowing will heal your heart and make you whole again.

Reason #10:
What doesn't kill you makes you... confident!

Franklin D. Roosevelt famously said, "The only thing we have to fear is fear itself." While he was referring at the time to the potential for widespread panic that could cripple the nation's economy, his wisdom applies on a day-to-day personal level, too.

The only thing many of us have to fear today is the fear of our own emotions. If we weren't terrified of our feelings, we wouldn't need to hide from them.

There are two reasons we hide from our feelings. The first is that they hurt, and we don't like to hurt. The second is what we think they mean. We're afraid of our "negative" feelings like envy, dislike, disappointment, frustration, etc., because we believe that having those emotions means we're envious, hateful, negative, weak people—in short, we're BAD!

No one tells us that good people do feel angry,

jealous, vengeful, irritated, impatient, and all those other uglies we try our best to hide. Good people feel all the emotions that humans are capable of. And, come to think of it, good people might be the ones who mostly have those bad emotions. If there are people in the world who are inherently bad, they probably don't feel especially bad inside. Research on psychopathy suggests, for example, that cold-blooded killers don't experience as much anxiety as normal people do.

The problem is we don't trust our own goodness. So for that reason, and because they hurt, we often try to hide from our "negative" emotions. Hiding from our own feelings makes us lose confidence in ourselves. How can you be confident in a self that can't stand to know the truth?

When you (w)allow in difficult feelings, you become less afraid, and not just of feelings. When you're not afraid of fear—or anger, despair, regret, etc.—you walk through life a more confident person. You know you can handle whatever comes your way in a typical day, even if you don't like it. Your emotions don't intimidate you; there's no need to be anxious about them.

If you can withstand your most painful feelings, even the really, really awful ones, you can weather just about anything.

Reason #11: Improve your relationships

What are your relationships based on? Is it doing things together? Sharing the same hobby, the same neighborhood, the same boss?

Do your relationships depend on your being helpful to the other person? Agreeing with everything they say? Giving or receiving advice?

When you think about the bonds that hold you close to the people in your life, how much has to do with sharing your emotional life with them? I don't mean talking about emotions ("I'm so mad at Debbie, I could spit!" "Tell me what happened." "Well, she called me up the other day and..."). I mean really sharing: *showing*, not just telling, what's important to you by letting others see your concern, your anger, your excitement, or your tears.

Relationships based on doing activities or sharing circumstances are held together by **situational bonds**. These can break when the situation breaks down. Ever changed jobs or addresses and lost friends when you left? Those were situational friends.

Relationships based on roles you play, like advice-giver, good listener, cheerleader, or helper, are held together by **contractual bonds**; there's an unspoken contract that binds you to act a certain way in the relationship. If you step outside your role too far, or for too long, these bonds can break.

Relationships based on acknowledging and respecting each other's feelings are held together by

emotional bonds. These are the most flexible and therefore the least likely to break if the situation changes. And there's no role playing, because each person gets to be him- or herself.

When you're tied to someone by emotional, rather than situational or contractual, bonds, you feel loved and respected for who you really are. You don't have to wonder why the other person likes you. They like who you are, because that's who you've presented to them. They know the real you, warts and all, and they like the person they know. What would be different in your life if all your relationships were based on that kind of bond?

Before you can feel safe bonding with another person like this, you need to feel safe within yourself to *be* yourself. (W)allowing in your emotions, especially with the support of a compassionate other person such as a counselor or friend, primes you for a new kind of relationship that doesn't rely on situations or role-playing. There may be people already in your life who would welcome the chance to share an emotional bond with you; if not, there are new potential friends waiting to meet you when you're ready.

Summary: Why wallow?

- You have no choice.
- It may be good for your health.
- Get your energy back.
- Enjoy the good things more.
- You're never more alone than when you abandon yourself.
- What we don't acknowledge controls us.
- You'll feel better sooner.
- It's natural.
- We all have something that needs healing.
- What doesn't kill you gives you confidence.
- It can improve your relationships.

Chapter 5

The T-R-U-T-H Technique

"Unbearable pain becomes its own cure."

~ GHALIB

Forty-nine-year-old Nola is a sales manager and marathon runner with a grown son who lives abroad. Her husband, a former contractor, is on disability and Nola is in charge of most of the household tasks. "Busy" is a good day for Nola; most days she's beyond busy, with barely enough time to go to the bathroom between work, chores, and training for her next race.

Nola was raised in the Midwest by people of Scandinavian heritage who were hearty, dependable, generous, and loyal, but also as tough as an arctic winter. Emotions were never discussed in public (or in private, if they could help it), and there was always a healthy nip of alcohol to soothe the troubled soul. In short, Nola was raised to deal with feelings by not dealing with them at all.

In our first therapy session, Nola told me she used to be happy but seemed to have lost that happiness, along with herself, somewhere along the way. A recent checkup found her to be in excellent health; there's no medical reason for her blue mood. Nola's nameless sadness is the focus of our work together.

Today Nola slumps in the client chair in my office, eyeing the Kleenex box. "I don't know what to do," she says in frustration. "I'm just so sick of feeling this way." I can see that she's battling a wave of tears, but so far her cheeks are dry.

"I just feel so..." Nola searches for the right word, then shrugs. "I don't know, maybe there's something wrong with my brain," she finishes.

I don't know whether there's something wrong with Nola's brain, but I do know that her way of dealing with feelings has set her up for exactly the sort of problem she's having now.

"You feel so...?" I prompt.

She's silent for a moment and then replies in a low voice, "Empty."

She loses the battle with her tears. One of them steals down her cheek before she can wipe it away. The air in the room is thick with her despair, and I can feel my own eyes becoming moist under the weight of it.

Nola's frustration erupts. "Whine, whine, whine. I don't know what to *do* about it!"

"It's painful to feel empty inside," I say. "It's so hard to sit with that emptiness."

Nola knows where I'm going with this and sighs in response. "But I've already done that. It doesn't work."

"What doesn't work?" I want to make sure I'm tracking her.

"Letting myself feel empty."

"What happens when you let yourself feel empty?"

"I let myself cry for a while, but then I just feel worse."

"How long do you cry before that happens?"

"Maybe five minutes."

"And what do you say to yourself at that point?"

She thinks for a moment. "That I'm pathetic. And possibly crazy. That I need to get a grip before my husband calls the loony bin to come and get me."

Whoa. Pretty harsh, right? One of the ongoing mysteries in my work is how people can believe that this kind of self-talk is a valid part of emotional healing. They seem to think that as long as they allow a little emotion to surface, a few tears to fall, they're cutting themselves enough slack and creating a healing environment. It doesn't seem to matter to them how they speak to themselves in response.

This is a fatal mistake, because self-criticism cancels out healing as surely as a tablespoon of salt ruins a bowl of vanilla pudding. If you criticize yourself while having your feelings, or set a time limit on self-compassion, you might as well pack up your wallowing kit, put it in the trunk and drive home, because you're finished before you even begin.

Whenever someone tells me they've been trying to (w)allow in their feelings but they're not getting anywhere, I can predict how they'll answer when I start asking for details. Self-criticism is always at the center of failed attempts to wallow constructively.

Nola's situation is typical of people I see. She wants to learn how to just allow herself to have her feelings, because not doing this has led her to where she is now. But when it comes right down to it, she isn't sure she can trust the feeling process, and so she puts boundaries around it. Since it was the attempt to put boundaries around feelings that got her into trouble to begin with, this only perpetuates the problem.

Self-Criticism:
As Effective as It Is Enjoyable

Like many of the people I work with, Nola confuses "having" feelings with "managing" feelings. (See Table 1 in Chapter 3). Though she thinks it's the painful feelings inside her that cause her continued suffering, the real source of her misery is her desire to avoid the painful feelings and her impatient attitude toward herself for not bucking up.

When Nola tells me she's tried just allowing herself to have her feelings, she's not being dishonest. She's convinced that she tried it exactly as prescribed. She thinks she allowed herself to feel because she let herself cry, and doesn't even notice how her self-criticism poisoned the process. Impatience with your own feelings is self-criticism in action.

When Nola gets frustrated with the process and wants to stop, it's as if she's saying to herself, "Aren't you done yet? This is taking too long. I've got other places I need to be, you know!" If you picture those words as coming at you from someone else when you're feeling bad, you'll notice they feel far more critical than supportive. How much better do you feel after hearing them?

Self-criticism is so stealthy, and so toxic to emotional healing, that uncovering it is one of the most important parts of the wallowing technique you'll learn in this chapter.

Managing feelings through self-criticism instead of having them is a national pastime. It's something we learn so early that we don't even know we're doing it.

What exactly does managing feelings this way look like? Typically, it goes something like this: A feeling arises, and instead of naming the feeling we think it through and find fault with ourselves, by saying things like...

"It's no big deal."

"I'm probably wrong about what she meant."

"I shouldn't worry about stuff like that."

"I'm too sensitive."

There's an endless list of things to think about and do instead of having our feelings. But that endless list is just a management tool to keep ourselves in line, and yucky feelings at bay.

By making a mental list of ways to look at the situation, or by acting out, we distract ourselves from feeling what we feel. Meanwhile, the actual emotion is sitting there going, "Hello? Can anyone hear me? Am I in the *room?*"

The management of feelings is, for many people, automatic and invisible. This explains why, when I talk with clients about feeling their feelings, I get the "been there, done that" response. People think that because they *reacted* to (i.e., thought about, criticized themselves for, or acted out) a feeling, they've felt the feeling. They believe that if they're suffering, it's because the feeling is still there.

Feeling an emotion is both easier and harder than managing an emotion. Easier because you don't have to fight reality. Harder because it's scary if you haven't done it before, it often hurts, and you have to let go of self-criticism to do it.

The first step to simply having a feeling is to notice your own resistance to feeling your emotions. It's the resistance to what already exists—your painful feelings—that causes suffering. If you can truly allow your feelings to just be whatever they are, a whole layer of "ouch" can be avoided. Alan W. Watts, in his timeless book *The Wisdom of Insecurity*, explains it like this: "Sometimes, when resistance ceases, the pain simply goes away or dwindles to an easily tolerable ache. At other times it remains, but the absence of any resistance brings about a way of feeling pain so unfamiliar as to be hard to describe. The pain is no longer *problematic*. I feel it, but there is no urge to get rid of it, for I have discovered that pain and the effort to be separate from it are the same thing." (Italics in original)

This process is what I refer to when I speak of "embracing" your feelings. To have a feeling, simply stop resisting the feeling. Name it if you can, and affirm that there's nothing wrong with feeling that way. The emotion itself will do the rest.

The Antidote: Self-Compassion

The most effective approach to painful feelings is one that enhances your compassion for yourself. Say kind things that a beloved friend might say, like...

"This is so hard, I feel for you"

"No wonder you're upset"

"I'm with you"

"You're very brave"

"I am so sorry for you"

How did you react to the statements in the list? If you don't like the thought of saying some of those things to yourself, what makes them distasteful to you? Is it easier for you to be kind and gentle to someone else? Imagine that you are someone who deserves a kind and gentle approach. Because you are. If you feel insincere when you're nice to yourself, see the question and answer on that topic in Chapter 9.

(W)allowing in feelings is *not* the time to pull yourself up by your bootstraps. Your own feelings need to matter to you. So much that you refuse to abandon yourself by ignoring them.

The recipe for having feelings, then, is first to note your resistance to feeling them, then name them if possible, then replace self-critical talk with self-compassionate talk while letting go of any resistance.

When you (w)allow in those feelings you'd rather not have, it's certainly going to hurt. That's why many of us would rather do just about anything than get in touch with our emotional pain. Before we get down on ourselves about that, let's agree that it's natural to avoid pain. It's the main reason, for example, that we don't willingly bend our knees and elbows backwards. Pain is Nature's way of warning us about things that are not good for us.

Emotional pain is similar to physical pain, in that it's a signal that something is wrong. But the pain itself is not wrong; it's only the messenger. When we refuse to (w)allow in our emotional pain, we're not avoiding trouble, we're shooting the messenger who's bringing news of trouble. And if we shoot the messenger, it's not going to keep delivering clear messages.

Our emotional pain tells us what's important to us. It tells us how well our lives suit us. And it tells us whether and when to change course. **Our emotional pain is not the problem. The situation we're in pain about is the problem.**

Clients of mine who have the courage to mentally cry "Ouch!" when life brings challenges large and small tell me that they feel more peaceful, authentic, and grounded, and less anxious. They've visited their pain in a spirit of acceptance. I can see it in their body language and hear it in their voices. They've reclaimed a piece of themselves that was buried with their pain, and they're stronger for it.

Change Your Life from the Inside Out

Theory is good, but practice is even better. What follows is a formal technique for (w)allowing in your difficult feelings and reclaiming your whole self.

The Technique is not a one-time fix but a blueprint for a new way of living. Learn it well and it will become a permanent part of you. It will change you forever. Once you've got the hang of it, you won't be able to go back to your old, inefficient ways of managing feelings, even if you wanted to. You won't constantly be on the lookout for tools for coping better, because coping won't be the issue it is now. Instead, with your emotions coming and going freely, you'll focus on expressing your highest purpose in life, the reason you're here.

But first, you must understand the Technique. And you must, of course, practice it.

The easiest way to learn the T-R-U-T-H Technique is by Vulcan mind-meld. That's how Mr. Spock often got information quickly from people on the original *Star Trek* TV show. He would form a psychic bridge between his mind and theirs, by putting his fingers on their heads and faces.

It was a highly efficient means of communication, since he would instantly know everything they knew. But since you and I can't do that (or at least *I* can't), I've broken the Technique down into a handy list of parts that can easily be printed in a book. I'm going to present these to you in a certain order, but in practice, all the steps happen at the same time. So please don't think of them as steps. Think of them as parts of the process, or pieces of a mechanical device that all work together simultaneously. As you read the description of the Technique, let it wash over you as a whole. Try to get a sense of the entire process before attempting to put it into practice.

Keeping your wallowing private—or contained in a safe space with a feelings-friendly therapist or other trusted companion—will help you feel safer and more comfortable. You're exploring a way to deal with painful feelings that may seem scary at first, so safety is important. If you're nervous, you might want to work through Chapter 8 first. It contains activities you can use to both warm up your "feeling muscles" and get centered in the present. These will build your comfort and confidence to use the Technique. If you still feel overwhelmed by your emotions after working through the exercises in Chapter 9, or cannot complete the exercises because of fear or anxiety, please seek the support of a qualified counselor or other mental health professional.

Expect to be a little bit awkward with the Technique when you start doing it. You've been doing things differently for a long time, and it will take effort and practice for you to adopt a new way of being. Please be patient with yourself.

You'll want to have the following supplies on hand if possible:

- A comfortable place to sit or lie down, if desired
- A full box of tissues
- At least one pillow

AVOID the following:
- Alcohol, food, or other distracting substances
- Computer, phone, or other communication devices
- Other people, unless you both know what you need

The T-R-U-T-H Technique

· ·

In case you didn't notice, the parts of the T-R-U-T-H Technique spell out the word "truth." Here are the five parts.

Tell yourself the situation.

Realize what you're feeling.

Uncover self-criticism.

Try to understand yourself.

Have the feeling.

Before you begin, breathe. Take your time. Take at least ten breaths. You don't need to do it in any special way; just breathe. Let your body relax. Here we go...

T: Tell yourself the situation

Keep it simple. Stick to the facts without evaluating them.

This can be harder than it sounds. You may have no idea why you feel the way you do. As we therapists love to say, THAT'S OKAY. In that case, just say, "I feel bad and I don't know why."

That's your truth. That's the situation as you know it.

If you know you feel just awful about a certain situation but don't know where to begin, say: "I feel awful about this whole thing with So-and-so."

Sometimes so much has happened that it's hard to sort out which part of it is making you feel what. Maybe you've been feeling anxious ever since you started a new relationship. But you also just found out your email account has been compromised and that your mother's blood pressure is dangerously high. Is it the relationship, the computer issues, or your mother's health that's stressing you out? Who knows? Just state the situation. You might simply say, "A lot has happened recently."

If you have a good idea what you're having feelings about, state the situation, keeping it as simple as possible.

Examples:
Someone has rejected you.
There's something coming up that you're not looking forward to.
Something important is beyond your control.
You've let yourself, or someone else, down.
You just feel bad, and you don't know why.

Breathe.
If your body feels tense, let it relax. Remember that nothing inside you can hurt you more than you've already been hurt.

R: Realize what you're feeling
What do you feel right this minute?
Don't go back to yesterday's feelings. Stay in this moment.

What are you feeling that you can wallow in right now? It's confession time. Tell yourself the truth. When it comes to your own emotions, let your motto be "Truth over beauty." Don't worry if your feelings aren't pretty. As long as they're your real feelings, they can heal you.

Try not to dwell on content. Your thoughts and feelings might be fused, making it hard for you just to be aware of an emotion. You may be replaying what happened, focusing on thoughts instead of feelings. Say to yourself, "I can't separate my feelings from my thoughts right now." And then say the magic words, AND THAT'S OKAY. Because it is.

You've just stated what you're aware of. If you're aware of a confusion of thoughts and feelings, that's what you're feeling right now: confusion. If you're aware of sadness but don't know the cause, that's what you're aware of right now: sadness.

There's no way you can get this wrong, as long you're paying attention to your experience.

There's no need to make sure your emotions are "correct" given the situation. You're allowed to have them, whatever they are, no matter what. Really! Trust for a moment that it's truly all right to have the feelings you have. It doesn't have to mean anything. Let go of judgment.

Crying over spilt milk? Go for it. You're allowed.

Feel your feelings with this sense of total freedom. Try to put words to any feelings you're experiencing. If you need some suggestions for feeling words, use Table 2 in Chapter 3.

Examples:

"I'm *dreading* my sister's wedding."
"I feel *hurt* by what he said, even if he didn't mean it that way."
"I'm *annoyed* at her for giving me advice I didn't ask for."
"I'm *afraid* of my own emotions. I don't want to look too closely."

Take some breaths, breathing into your real feelings. Notice any tension in your body. You can let it go. You're safe right now, emotionally.

U: Uncover self-criticism

We criticize ourselves to make ourselves better people, but the self-criticism just makes us feel bad. And then we criticize ourselves again for feeling bad! It's a negative feedback loop. It doesn't help. It only hurts, and makes us want to hide the truth from ourselves.

So check yourself: Are you doing this exercise only to appease what seems like a childish part of you? Are you hoping that doing this will silence that part so you can move forward without its pulling on your sleeve all the time? If so, you're coming from a place of self-criticism, and you'll end up back where you started, frustrated with yourself and your feelings.

Uncover that self-criticism! Don't let it lurk in the shadows, getting in your way. You must take note of the subtle and not-so-subtle ways you undermine your own healing.

Examples of self-criticism:

Impatience with feelings
Insistence on feelings being accurate or justified
Prioritizing "moving forward" over knowing and loving
    yourself better

Examples of self-critical thoughts:

"I shouldn't feel that way; she's my only sister."
"I'm too sensitive."
"I'm such a hypocrite."
"Why am I making a big deal out of this tiny thing?"
"A normal person would have gotten over this by now."
"There must be something wrong with me."

You're not so bad that you have to be kept in line all the time. You can safely drop the self-criticism. I'll give you something to replace it with. Keep breathing.

Instead of criticizing...

T: Try to understand yourself

Instead of evaluating your feelings as good or bad, or yourself as good or bad for having the feelings you do, put your brain to work on understanding yourself. Somebody ought to try to see things from your point of view. Why not you?

In a comic scene from an old movie called *Spies Like Us,* two bungling would-be spies pose as doctors and end up performing a surgical demonstration. Met with skepticism from the real surgeons who are observing, one of impostors replies with haughty authority, "We mock what we don't understand."

There's truth in that last statement. When we demean or ridicule ourselves for having certain emotions, it's often because we really don't understand why we feel the way we do. The flip side—and the good news—is that anything you can understand, you can have compassion for.

Understanding your feelings, however, is sometimes easier said than done. So many emotions may have been tangled together inside of you for so long that you don't even know where to start. And you know what? Say it with me: THAT'S OKAY. You don't *have* to know exactly why you feel the way you do. Some feelings have roots that go so far back, it's unlikely you'd remember the original trigger. Remember: Old feelings and newer feelings can become entwined. It can be easier to navigate the U.S. Patent Office than to get a handle on exactly why you feel a certain way.

All you have to know is this: You have good reasons for feeling the way you do. If you could pinpoint each trigger, your feelings would make perfect sense to you.

You've already identified a situation and a feeling. Now take a step back and ask yourself, *Why* might a good person feel this way? Don't evaluate whether you think a good person *should* feel this way. Just find an explanation that makes sense. Find a cause to say, "No wonder I feel this way."

Once you think of a reason—any reason—why a good person in your situation might feel exactly as you do, you can speak kind and encouraging words to yourself, either out loud or in your thoughts. Finding the perfect or most accurate explanation is not the point here. The purpose of seeking understanding is to soften your stance and allow some compassion to enter your heart.

Here are a few examples:

"The wedding will take a lot out of me. There's so much work to be done. I'm tired.... No wonder I'm not looking forward to it."

"I've been hurt in just that way before. He poked a tender spot in me.... No wonder I feel hurt."

"I grew up feeling incompetent. When someone offers me advice, it makes me feel incompetent all over again, and I hate that! No wonder I was so annoyed."

"I've been a stranger to myself for so long, I'm worried about what I might find if I look inside. There's probably a lot of pain there.... No wonder I'm scared."

This is called validation. You need it right now. You deserve it. Give it to yourself.

Breathe...

H: Have the feeling

If, at this point, you're still suffering with difficult emotions, allow them to be inside you. Allow yourself to really wallow in them. Remember that, when you're wallowing, what you're really doing is *allowing*. And that's a beautiful thing, because it means you're becoming whole again in this moment.

There's nothing you need to do about your feelings right now. Just sit with them. Cry if you feel like it, hug or punch a pillow. If you speak to yourself, speak only kind words. As you experience your true feelings, let them matter to you as if you were your own dear friend.

CONSTRUCTIVE SURRENDER

"At fifteen life had taught me undeniably that surrender, in its place, was as honorable as resistance, especially if one had no choice."

~ **MAYA ANGELOU**

"Healing doesn't take place until we surrender to our feelings and allow them to wash over us."

~ **CHRISTIANE NORTHRUP, M.D.**

"The best thing one can do when it's raining is to let it rain."

~ **HENRY WADSWORTH LONGFELLOW**

"We deem those happy who, from the experience of life, have learned to bear its ills, without being overcome by them."

~ **JUVENAL**

"Everything has its wonders, even darkness and silence, and I learn, whatever state I may be in, therein to be content."

~ **HELEN KELLER**

"There are lots of ways of being miserable but there's only one way of being comfortable, and that is to stop running around after happiness."

~ **EDITH WHARTON**

"What could be more futile, more insane, than to create inner resistance to what already is?"

~ **ECKHART TOLLE**

"The creative process is a process of surrender, not control."

~ **JULIA CAMERON**

Make It Work for You

When I worked in television promotion, it was popular to speak of products that had great appeal as "sexy." The T-R-U-T-H Technique *isn't* sexy. It's not necessarily fun, and you might find yourself getting bored. You might feel a pull to go back to managing, rather than having, your feelings. Managing is familiar, and whatever's familiar always seems easier—even when it's not.

While you're practicing the Technique, however, stay alert to managing your emotions, and fight against the temptation to think instead of feel. We've talked about the difference between having and managing emotions. If you're doing a lot of thinking, worrying, or playing out scenes in your head, you're managing. Bring yourself back to experiencing the feelings. Your quality of life depends on it.

It's hard to stop managing and just *feel*, isn't it? Sometimes the best you can do is to notice you're managing your feelings instead of having them. Give yourself a lot of leeway; the learning curve can be steep.

Tips for Dealing with Sadness, Anger or Fear

It might or might not be obvious, but embracing a feeling is something you can do only if you're having a feeling right in this moment.

If you're not feeling anything right now, there's nothing for you to embrace. You can't hug a person if they're in Paris and you're in Pittsburgh. One of you has to get on a plane and get to the same geographic space for an embrace to happen. Otherwise, you'll be hugging air.

The Technique creates space for your feelings so they can get on that tiny plane inside and come to visit you. If they don't, they don't. That's their prerogative. You haven't done anything wrong. Just acknowledge, "I'm not in touch with my feelings right now." And you know the rest... (Hint: It has to do with whether IT'S OKAY.)

It's all okay. It really is. Remember, "allow" is most of the word "wallow." Whatever happens, happens. This is a private, personal time; no one is here to criticize you. You can safely experience this moment.

If tears want to come, let them come. Don't try to stop them. Don't suck them back in. Crying is an effective coping mechanism, not a sign of weakness. Emotional crying may release endorphins (feel-good chemicals) that alleviate pain and stress, and tears contain stress hormones you could definitely do without. Crying tears of emotion can literally make you feel better. So go ahead and cry, no matter what the reason.

Remember to avoid judgment. Breathe. Allow your body to relax. You already survived the original injury that may still be causing you pain, and you can survive the feeling it triggered. Allow your tears to help heal that wound.

If anger shows up, let 'er rip! Good people can and

do get angry. There's nothing to be afraid of. Just don't hurt any living thing in the name of anger. That's not wallowing, that's acting out.

Anger is one of those feelings that wants to get physical. You can scream into a pillow if you feel like screaming. You can also moan, growl, roar, wail, curse, or use gibberish to express your rage. Turn the pillow into a punching bag if you want to pummel something. Set up an area where you can safely break things. Get yourself some second-hand dishes and a pair of safety goggles, and go to town. If you're mobile and accustomed to exercise, you can go for a run, jump up and down, or do push-ups to help the feeling move through you.

If anger comes up for you often, an exercise program could be a great help in working through it. Just make sure to get the thumbs-up from your doctor before starting, especially if you haven't exercised for a while or you have health concerns.

Anger can be a cover for softer feelings like hurt and sadness. Don't be surprised if, when your anger is spent, you feel sad. Whatever the reason for your anger, don't criticize yourself. You're allowed to be angry. There's no such thing as a "wrong" reason for any feeling. No one gets hurt just by your having a feeling, even if that feeling is anger. Feel the anger, rather than acting it out. You can decide later if you want to do something about it. For now, it's nobody's business but yours.

If you feel afraid, acknowledge the fear. Give yourself a hug and let yourself know that you're there for you. Don't abandon yourself in your hour of need. Telling yourself not to be ridiculous is not healing, not productive, and not kind. Avoid talking yourself out of it or trying to make yourself feel better. Just be afraid if you're afraid, and open your mind to understanding what the fear is about.

Please don't think that, by comforting yourself, you're giving up on ever getting comfort from someone else. It doesn't work that way. If you can't comfort yourself, you will not be able to receive comfort from others on a deep level. It's not an "either/or," but everything starts with you. Learn to receive by giving to yourself. It will help you receive from others.

Your fear may be very old. It may come from a time when you felt you were in danger. At the time, you didn't know what to do with the fear, so it got buried. Now it's surfacing. It just needs to be acknowledged and allowed to exist within you. It doesn't want to be there inside you forever. But it's there now, and it needs your attention. Watch the movie of your fear, and let it play to the end.

If you're safe now, remind yourself with compassion that you're safe now. But don't try to shut the door on the fear. If it's not directly caused by a physical condition, it will diminish over time with your embrace. If your fear is based in present circumstances, it will go away when the situation becomes less scary. Until then, it's appropriate to be afraid. Don't blame your fear. Blame the situation that scares you.

Underneath those yucky feelings of sadness, anger, or fear is very often the yuckiest one of all: shame.

Shame tells us we're basically wrong or bad as people. Since that's an intensely uncomfortable feeling, we try to ignore it. And some of us succeed so well, we're not even aware of our shame. It controls us without our knowledge. It creates a continuous experience of low self-esteem, along with all that that entails.

It's unfortunate, because you can't change what you don't know about. If you feel bad a lot of the time, and you aren't sure why, you may be suffering from chronic shame.

Try on this statement: "I feel ashamed of myself."

What happens for you?

Maybe you agree with that statement but don't know why.

Maybe you can't bring yourself to say it.

Maybe it makes you mad to say it.

Maybe you feel nothing as you say it.

Maybe you fall asleep as you think about saying it.

Maybe you just feel horrible.

No matter what the feeling, the rule for healing doesn't change: If there's an emotion inside you, you must feel it if you want to regain a sense of control and confidence.

However awful the emotion you're embracing, hang on to it for as long as you can. Try to beat the world record for Longest Embrace of a Painful Feeling. Remember: You let feelings "go" by feeling them fully. Once they're felt, they can leave.

If you feel better immediately after using the Technique, your wallowing has been constructive and healing has taken place. Even so, there may be much more healing that wants to happen. You didn't get to where you are overnight, and you won't heal overnight. Set some time and space aside to use the Technique every time you have an opportunity to sit with a significant feeling. Let it become your new way of dealing with emotional pain.

If you feel worse immediately after wallowing, you may be stuck on one of the parts of the process. From what I can tell, it's the middle one—uncovering self-criticism—that's the hardest for most people. Judging yourself and your feelings can seem like a part of who you are.

If you feel better immediately afterwards but worse a few hours or days later, what you're experiencing is normal. Tapping into feelings can be like kicking up dust. Things don't settle back down right away. Think of this as a side effect that will go away with consistent use of the Technique. Meanwhile, wallow in the dust when it comes up.

The Secret to Your Success

In acting class, I learned that in order to be believable as a character, an actor must completely commit to the role. When you're onstage delivering a performance, if even 1 percent of you is holding back, the entire performance will lack credibility. In wallowing, as in acting, even the smallest lack of commitment can ruin an otherwise healing experience. When you're having feelings, you must be entirely on board with allowing yourself to feel the way you do, with empathy. Otherwise, you can cry all day long, and it's as if you never cried at all. Instead of healing, you're just hurt again. The healing can happen only if you maintain a steady attitude of caring toward yourself. Don't be discouraged; practice will make perfect. Enlist the help of someone committed to your well-being if you need it.

When using the Technique, keep your mind on the task of understanding yourself. Refuse to budge from your own side. Don't evaluate your emotions, just think of a reason that they might be there. This kind of self-compassion is a powerful force for healing and change.

In the next chapter, I'll show you what it looks like to use the Technique.

Summary

- Self-criticism is the enemy of healing; replace it with self-compassion.
- To have a feeling, notice resistance to it and let that go.
- To wallow constructively, use the T-R-U-T-H Technique:
  - o Tell yourself the situation. (Keep it as simple as possible.)
  - o Realize what you're feeling. (Name the feeling[s] if you can.)
  - o Uncover self-criticism. (Root out impatience or lack of kindness toward yourself.)
  - o Try to understand yourself. (Look for reasons that a good person would feel this way.)
  - o Have the feeling (and let it matter to you).
- Accept and allow whatever comes up for you when trying the Technique; it's all okay.
- For the process to work, you must commit to it fully.

Chapter 6

Constructive Wallowing in Action

From everyday annoyances to life-changing trag-edies, (w)allowing in our feelings helps us work through difficulties large and small. No situation is too much, or too minor, for the T-R-U-T-H Technique.

The following case studies show how the Technique can be used effectively in a variety of situations.

The Inconsiderate Neighbor

Meet Tony. A successful computer engineer, he recently bought his first house, at the age of 27. He loves his new home, but he's unhappy about the fact that his next-door neighbor keeps an unsightly pile of junk right on the property line between their houses.

The pile has been growing since Tony moved in two months ago, and today he decides to go over and talk to his neighbor about it.

Tony is nervous as he approaches the front steps; this will be their first face-to-face meeting.

The neighbor takes a while to appear at the door, and when she does, she looks wary.

"Hi," says Tony, as pleasantly as he can. "I'm Tony, your new neighbor."

"What do you need?" asks the neighbor bluntly. Tony wasn't expecting a response like this. He decides to plunge ahead.

"Well, I was just noticing that there's a pile of...stuff between our houses," he says, pointing vaguely toward his own house.

The neighbor waits for him to continue. Tony isn't sure what to say next.

"...And I was just wondering...if you could...um... move it?" Tony already wishes he could start again.

"Where do you want me to move it to?"

Again, Tony didn't anticipate this. He tries to come up with other places on her property where it might be moved to, none of which meet with her approval.

Tony is stumped. "I guess that's the only place it can be," he concedes, and he's immediately angry with himself for doing so.

"Yeah, pretty much," she shrugs.

She looks like she's got other things to attend to, and Tony has no idea where to go from here, so he says, "Okay. Thanks for your time." Kicking himself mentally, he goes back to his house.

Ten minutes later, pacing his living room, Tony can't stop thinking about what happened. He doesn't like how he feels, and he's trying to figure out what to do.

Whenever we're in the grip of unpleasant feelings, and can't seem to think about anything else, that's the perfect time to practice the Technique from the last chapter.

Everyone has a different history, temperament and personality; you and I might not feel exactly the same way Tony feels right now. The important thing for Tony is to embrace the truth about what he's feeling, not how someone else might feel.

Let's go through the T-R-U-T-H Technique with Tony and find out what's going on in his heart and mind as he struggles to deal with his churning emotions.

Tony sits down and takes a few breaths before he begins. He tries to relax his tense body but has a hard time doing it. He's really keyed up. He takes a few breaths and thinks about the five pieces of the Technique. His thoughts are in italics below.

T: Tell yourself the situation

I went over to talk to my neighbor about the junk pile, and she blew me off.

R: Realize what you're feeling

Mad at her
Mad at myself
Regretful
Humiliated

U: Uncover self-criticism

I was such a wimp!

I shouldn't care about the pile anyway. What a petty thing to care about.

I shouldn't be so upset about what happened; it's not the end of the world.

I shouldn't have unkind thoughts about my neighbor.

T: Try to understand yourself

I feel like I blew it, my one and only chance to talk to her about it. Now it seems like I'm stuck with that pile AND a tense relationship with my neighbor. No wonder I regret what happened.

H: Have the feeling

[Tony realizes that his strongest feeling right this moment is regret.]

I regret that interaction so much! I regret, regret, REGRET it. I wish I could do it over again. I wish it had been different. I regret it. I regret how I handled that.

As he embraces the discomfort, really gets inside his regret, Tony feels himself becoming more calm. He has labeled and is now fully experiencing the feeling; now, instead of feeling vaguely "bad," or impotently angry at his neighbor for her behavior, he feels regretful.

He (w)allows in the regret, saying "I regret how I handled that" over and over until the truth of it surrounds him. The regret is pure; it's not tinged with self-criticism.

Tony has embraced his feelings, and nothing bad

has happened. The house didn't cave in on him. There was no thunderbolt from the sky. And he feels better, not worse. He's not managing or struggling with his feelings. He's just having them.

Notice that Tony is simply embracing the regret that is already there; he's not creating or intensifying the regret by focusing on it. The regret is the same whether he focuses on it or not. But now, instead of getting buried and impacted inside him, that unpleasant feeling can move through him and dissipate naturally. **By allowing himself to feel the regret, Tony is literally letting it go.**

A few minutes later, now that his most painful feeling has been fully felt, Tony discovers that he feels better; the regret has passed for now. He finds himself thinking about what to have for dinner.

Tony will return to the question of what to do about his neighbor and the pile at another time. For now, the need to obsess about their conversation has gone away. Obsessions like that are fueled by unacknowledged feelings, but Tony has acknowledged his.

Sure, he may have more problems with his neighbor, and more feelings later. When he thinks about their meeting today, he might feel regret again. Emotions tend to come in waves, especially when experiences are fresh.

It's important to understand that Tony won't feel his regret any more strongly, or any longer, than he would if he'd refused to wallow in it. Over hours or days, he will successfully let it go. And once this particular regret is gone, it will never come back to nibble at his heart.

Will he feel regret again? Certainly. Will he ever

feel this particular wave of regret again? No way. This one has left the building.

Constructive wallowing is not a one-time solution, but a way of life. If Tony keeps the lines of communication open between himself and his feelings, he'll continue to be emotionally whole and healthy, even when life sends him junk piles.

If your current way of managing emotions is to ignore unpleasant feelings, your heart might need some spring cleaning. Using the T-R-U-T-H Technique will allow you to really let go of negative feelings, maybe for the first time.

While Tony enjoys a peaceful dinner of linguine with vegetables and a nice glass of wine, let's look in on a few more people who are using the Technique to deal with their difficult feelings. The more you see it in action, the more comfortable you'll be with using the Technique yourself.

A Disappointing Vacation

Three weeks after a Spring Break vacation in Mexico, college sophomore Rachel finds herself struggling with some troubling feelings about the trip. The two friends she went with, Alana and Brittany, clearly had a wonderful time, and all three have told everyone that the trip was fun. But Rachel feels a tension between herself and them since they returned.

From the minute they arrived at the Mexican hotel

and unpacked their suitcases, it was clear that Alana and Brittany had different ideas than Rachel about how to have a good time. Out came the high heels and party dresses. Rachel's suitcase, in contrast, contained a bathing suit, flip-flops, a fully stocked e-book reader, suntan lotion, shorts, sneakers, and every T-shirt she owned.

Rachel works hard during the school year, so she was looking forward to enjoying large chunks of unstructured time, lying in the sun, reading, and swimming. She was also hoping to spend some quality friend-time with Alana and Brittany talking for hours about school, men, and life back home. However, the other girls had a different agenda: dance all night, meet men, sleep late, and fit in some shopping whenever possible.

The result was that Rachel spent most of her vacation alone, going to the movies once but otherwise fending for herself near the hotel. Alana and Brittany were sorry that Rachel hadn't packed any party clothes, but they couldn't seem to stay out of the clubs for even one night or get up early even one day to spend time with their book-loving, T-shirted friend.

Rachel tells herself that the trip is over, it had its high points (at least the outbound plane ride was fun), and it's time to move on. Next time she goes anywhere with friends, she'll pack some nicer clothes in case she wants to go out.

But even though she wants to focus on the positive and let the rest go, her feelings continue to bother her. She knows wallowing will help her get past what she's feeling and into a better space, so she decides to give it a try. Here is Rachel's T-R-U-T-H sheet.

T: Tell yourself the situation

My friends basically ignored me on our vacation.

R: Realize what you're feeling

Hurt
Mad at them for abandoning me
Mad at myself for not packing nicer clothes
Anxious about losing them as friends

U: Uncover self-criticism

I shouldn't be so negative; the trip wasn't terrible.
I should have known better.
It's no use dwelling on the past.
If I don't like what happened, why haven't I talked to them about it?

T: Try to understand yourself

I packed for the vacation I wanted to have. It didn't occur to me that Alana and Brittany would want to go out every night. They don't do that here. How was I supposed to know?

I spent Spring Break basically alone. I feel rejected by my friends. No wonder I'm upset.

Alana and Brittany are important to me, and I don't want to lose them. So it makes sense that I feel so bad about all this.

H: Have the feeling

I feel BAD. It's hard to tell sometimes which anger is at me and which is at them. A lot of it feels like anger at myself. I feel bad about myself. I feel like I ruined the trip for all of us, but at the same time I resent them for abandoning me. I'm trying to just feel the bad instead of trying to make it better. This is hard. I keep thinking about what I should do about it, instead of just allowing myself to feel bad. Wow—I'm afraid they don't like me anymore. I didn't realize I was afraid of that, but I am. I'm worried they think I'm boring.

Rachel uses the Technique to sort through a number of feelings and tease apart a couple of different factors at play. She was confused at first because she wasn't sure whom to be angry at about what happened—herself or her friends. In spending some time with her feelings she found that underneath it all was a fear of losing them.

There's no cure for this kind of separation anxiety; we're hard-wired to suffer when our established social bonds threaten to break. But knowing what her feelings are and why they're there helps Rachel to focus on what's happening right now.

If she hadn't taken the time to explore her internal landscape and discover her fear of losing the friendship, that anxiety would probably continue to control her behavior around Alana and Brittany, making the existing tension worse. But, because the fear is now conscious, she doesn't have to be controlled by it. Instead, Rachel can ask herself some new questions and listen carefully to the answers.

How much does she still want to be friends with Alana and Brittany? Does she want or need to talk with them about what happened on vacation? What is her friendship with these women based on, and is that what she wants her friendships to be based on?

Rachel may have other questions for herself. She has somewhere to go with this now.

A Loved One with a Scary Diagnosis

Mark and Evelyn have been married for thirty years. Evelyn was recently diagnosed with colon cancer following a routine examination. Surgery to remove part of her colon has been scheduled. Her prognosis is good, since the cancer was caught early, but Mark is shocked and disturbed by her diagnosis.

T: Tell yourself the situation

My wife has cancer and has to have surgery.

R: Realize what you're feeling

Frustrated

Scared

Helpless

Mad at myself for not protecting her

Mad at myself for feeling scared when I should be a rock for her

Mad at her for getting cancer (?)

U: Uncover self-criticism

I'm not a good husband.

I'm a coward.

It's self-indulgent for me to wallow in worry when

she's the one who's going through this.

I'm just making myself feel bad by thinking about it.

Her prognosis is good, so I should be thankful it's not worse.

I shouldn't blame her for getting cancer! That's crazy!

T: Try to understand yourself

My wife is the most important person in my life. It's normal to have feelings about her having any kind of cancer. No wonder I'm so emotional right now. Who wouldn't be? I love her and it's natural to want to protect her, even when I can't. My anger just shows how much I love her, how scared and helpless I feel. Anger feels better than those other feelings. It feels more powerful somehow. It's just my way of coping.

H: Have the feeling

Damn her for this! How could she do this to us?...It hurts so much to think of losing her. I don't want to think about it. I want to go to sleep until this is over. I guess I'm ashamed of myself for not wanting to deal with this. I feel really ashamed. I'm even ashamed of being scared. I'm so ashamed. Oh God, now I'm crying, and now I'm even more ashamed. I'm miserable. This is so hard. How am I supposed to be there for her when I can barely keep myself together? And when I feel so angry about all this? This is the worst of it, I think. I'm in the pit of despair... and yet I'm still breathing. This is what it feels like to hit bottom. I'm still breathing.

Mark is having a dark night of the soul, triggered by Evelyn's diagnosis and the thought of losing her. The compassion he finds for himself during this session is crucial; it's what will enable him to be there for her. If he didn't acknowledge and forgive himself for his irrational anger toward his wife, his ability to support her emotionally would be compromised. He'd have to try to hide the anger from both her and himself, which would keep him from being present; his worry would come true, and he wouldn't be able to "be her rock" as he wants to.

Using the Technique, he neutralized the threat of the anger by treating it with compassion; now it doesn't have to be hidden, so it won't keep him from being wholly present for her.

He's also given himself the chance to receive the attention and empathy that he, too, deserves. He's not just a bystander here. His life as he knows it is threatened. Who knows how long this ordeal will last? It's important that Mark continue to allow himself to visit with his own feelings going forward, so as not to allow a backlog to build.

"I Can't Get Over What Happened"

Remember Natasha, the forestry student from the Introduction? She lost the use of her legs in a car accident while riding her bike to school. Two years later, she's still depressed. In fact, she's more than depressed, as she discovers when she uses the T-R-U-T-H Technique.

She completes the Technique with the help and support of a counselor she's been working with.

T: Tell yourself the situation

I was hit by a drunk driver and my legs will never work again.

R: Realize what you're feeling

Angry!!!
Frustrated with myself
Sad
(But mostly angry!!!)

U: Uncover self-criticism

Anger is draining and toxic; good people shouldn't be angry.

Do I really want to feel this way forever? Why hang on to this?

It's been two years—I should at least TRY to forgive the person who hit me.

T: Try to understand yourself

I guess it's normal to be angry when your life is changed against your will. I tried for so long not to be angry, but the anger just stayed inside me while I tried to positive-think it away. That's why it's here now. I never really felt it fully. It makes sense to be angry. It's obviously a huge thing to lose the use of your legs. I have a right to feel the way I do.

H: Have the feeling

I'm furious at that stupid driver!!! She stole my life from me!!! I feel so incredibly, incredibly...sad. I used to run in the forest, jumping over fallen logs. I used to climb trees and ford streams.... I pictured walking down the aisle in a gorgeous white dress when I got married. I'll never have that now. I'm lost. I'm so lost and just so SAD I can't even find words. This just hurts so deeply. I hurt. I hurt.... I hate her! I HATE that driver!!!!!!!!!... And now all the feelings have drained away from me. How odd.

The unfairness of what happened to Natasha is almost intolerable, and anger is the only rational response. Even though it won't bring back the use of her legs, it is completely understandable.

But there's even more to Natasha's suppressed anger than meets the eye. Like many people I've met, she spent the first eighteen years of her life living in a family of people who rarely expressed anger. There was an unspoken rule in Natasha's family that anger should be neither seen nor heard. "We're all nice people here, and nice people don't get angry," was the implicit message. So when Natasha got mad for any reason, even before the accident, it was like that old song from *Sesame Street*: "One of these things just doesn't belong here." It was the anger that didn't belong, and so it was usually stuffed away instead of fully experienced—a dirty little secret not to be dwelt upon, let alone revealed.

Now that Natasha is successfully accessing and expelling her suppressed anger, she's got access not just to her feelings about the accident but also about everything else that's ever made her mad. The accident is a focal point for her anger, and it's a good one. It's comparatively easy for Natasha to be angry about something as significant as losing certain physical abilities. Even still, it takes mental effort for her to be okay with feeling as angry as she does.

The anger comes in waves, like other emotions. This provides Natasha with natural rest periods like the one that occurs toward the end of her session above.

The more sessions Natasha can have like this one, the more relief she'll obtain and the sooner she'll come out from under the weight of her anger. Also, she'll begin to experience more frequent and deeper moments of pleasure, because the pathway to all her feelings has been opened by her willingness to have her anger.

Midlife Crisis

Let's return to Nola, from the beginning of Chapter 5. A busy marathon runner, she started therapy because of a painful feeling of emptiness at midlife. After several counseling sessions, the emptiness has shifted, and now Nola is aware of an intense sadness and a longing to reconnect with her authentic self. The shift from feeling empty to feeling sad occurred because Nola's willingness to connect with the emptiness created a bridge to her inner world. Once that bridge was built, Nola had access to more of her feelings—along with the parts of herself that she was missing.

TO KNOW YOU
IS TO LOVE YOU

"Today you are You, that is truer than true. There is no one alive who is Youer than You."

~ DR. SEUSS

"Knowing yourself is the beginning of all wisdom."

~ ARISTOTLE

"Who looks outside, dreams. Who looks inside, awakes."

~ CARL JUNG

"Be yourself; everyone else is already taken."

~ OSCAR WILDE

"Insist on yourself. Never imitate."

~ RALPH WALDO EMERSON

"Find out who you are and do it on purpose."

~ DOLLY PARTON

"First of all, it's a hell of a responsibility to be yourself. It's much easier to be somebody else or nobody at all."

~ SYLVIA PLATH

"We shall not cease from exploration/And the end of all our exploring/Will be to arrive where we started/And know the place for the first time."

~ T.S. ELIOT

While it may be a toss-up as to which feels worse—emptiness or sadness—the goal is to heal by integrating lost emotions into a whole self. This is done, as we know, by embracing them. Following your pain as it transforms and goes deeper is a good way to access parts of yourself that were previously hidden.

This wallowing session is a snapshot of Nola on a single day in her life. If she continues to use this tool over time, she will likely continue to experience emotional shifts on her way to wholeness and health.

T: Tell yourself the situation

I've lost my way and I don't know who I am.

R: Realize what you're feeling

Grief

Sadness

Regret

Longing

Embarrassment

Hope

U: Uncover self-criticism

People my age should already know who they are.

I have a good life; I should be happy with what I've got.

I need to stop whining and get over this.

T: Try to understand yourself

Everything might look okay from the outside, but everything is not okay with me. I don't regret having my son or marrying my husband, but I do think I lost myself along the way while I was being there for my family and everyone else. I was taught to put other people's needs ahead of my own. I do it so well that I barely know how to pay attention to what I want or need. How can I know myself if I don't ever pay attention to me? The grief I feel is for all the times I ignored myself. As well as the opportunities I passed up to know myself better, or to do things I thought I might be good at or enjoy. No wonder I feel such a loss. I'm not asking for anything extraordinary. It's okay to want to know who I am. I want my family to know themselves, too.

H: Have the feeling

I regret all the times I ignored my own needs when I really didn't have to. I let myself down. I wish I'd been there for myself more. I'm sad and I'm sorry. And I'm angry that I'll never get those years back. I am in mourning for what I've lost.... I'm embarrassed by my pain. Where I come from, people don't do pain. They suck it up and keep moving. But I'm tired of doing that.

And now all of a sudden, I feel hopeful...

And now I'm sad again. A whirlwind of feelings, and I don't know where they start or end. Sadness now. Bitter tears, regret. Feeling sleepy all of a sudden. Curiously peaceful and more in touch with...something. Hope.

If it's been years since you've had a heart-to-heart with yourself, there's bound to be an awful lot to look at and feel. Grief is not at all unusual, but there's another feeling, too. I don't know what to call it, but I feel it when

I see a tearful reunion between a mother and child, or two siblings who were separated at birth. It's a response to an intensely emotional experience. It's both happy and sad at the same time. It's indescribable.

I think there's a version of that same feeling that occurs inside you when you finally come home to yourself. Nola is a person who has a full life on paper—marriage, motherhood, a home, a career—but that's all on paper. Having been raised to stuff her emotions, Nola is surviving but not really *living*. She's now using the Technique to heal from being separated from her own heart, and to thaw her emotional machinery so she can feel what it's like to truly live.

Your Turn

None of these people died of their feelings, and all are experiencing a shift of some kind through adopting the practice of telling themselves the truth. Are you ready to practice with some feelings of your own? Use the T-R-U-T-H Technique Worksheet on pages 153-154 or, if privacy is a concern, make one of your own. I recommend writing down your responses when you first start using the T-R-U-T-H Technique. This will be easier than trying to keep track of your thoughts during the first four parts of the process.

When you come to "Have the feeling," you don't need to write anything at all. Writing invites you to intellectualize your experience instead of just having it.

So instead of writing, have the feeling. Name the feeling if you can, but otherwise, just listen to your heart.

Good luck, and remember: Nothing inside you can hurt you more than you've already been hurt. If you start to feel overwhelmed, use the grounding exercise in Chapter 8.

Try going through the parts of the T-R-U-T-H Technique in your head every time you have a small emotional reaction, good or bad, as you go about your day. In a short time you'll be a master wallower who can do all of them together. Before breakfast.

The T-R-U-T-H Technique Worksheet

Write your thoughts in the blanks provided in parts 1 through 4. For Part 5, just experience your emotions with self-compassion until they pass.

T: Tell yourself the situation (in one sentence).

R: Realize what you're feeling. (Use feeling words.)

U: Uncover self-criticism. (Look for "should" language, e.g., "I shouldn't feel this way.")

T: Try to understand yourself. (Why might a good person feel this way?)

H: Have the feeling. (And let it matter to you. Be kind.)

PART III

Float Like a
Butterfly

Chapter 7

The Daunting Dozen: Top Twelve Wallowing Worries

How did it go when you tried the T-R-U-T-H Technique? Did you bump up against any of the self-critical thoughts voiced by Tony and the others in the last chapter?

The thoughts and worries they expressed in the "Uncover self-criticism" part of the T-R-U-T-H Technique are all too common, and it does take courage and a leap of faith to overcome them. So how about we take a tour of the concerns voiced by our five brave wallowers in the last chapter?

COURAGE

"Touch a thistle timidly and it pricks you; grasp it boldly and its spines crumble."

~ **ADMIRAL WILLIAM HALSEY**

"A man with outward courage dares to die; a man with inner courage dares to live."

~ **LAO TZU**

"Courage is rightly esteemed the first of human qualities...because it is the quality which guarantees all others."

~ **WINSTON CHURCHILL**

"Life shrinks or expands in proportion to one's courage."

~ **ANAÏS NIN**

"Nothing in life is to be feared, it is only to be understood. Now is the time to understand more, so that we may fear less."

~ **MARIE CURIE**

"We could never learn to be brave and patient if there were only joy in the world."

~ **HELEN KELLER**

"He has not learned the lesson of life who does not every day surmount a fear."

~ **RALPH WALDO EMERSON**

"Your willingness to wrestle with your demons will cause your angels to sing. Use the pain as fuel, as a reminder of your strength."

~ **AUGUST WILSON**

I'd like to fill in the blanks and address the errors that underlie these worries, so you can rest assured that it's safe and healthy to move forward with this new wallowing lifestyle.

There are other, equally common, worries addressed in the "Questions & Answers" section of Chapter 9, so be sure to search there as well if your worry isn't listed here.

Worry #1: My feelings might be wrong

Have you ever been upset with someone, or felt bad about an interaction, but you weren't sure whether you were right to feel the way you did? If so, you might have "obsessed" about it for hours or days, turning the situation over and over in your mind, looking for a way to understand it that might make the picture clearer. You wanted to know if you were right to feel the way you did.

If you're like most people, you skewed the replay to make yourself either totally right or totally wrong. But either way, replaying the situation in your mind like this remained unsatisfying, no matter how many times you did it.

We can never be sure of the Truth about any interaction between ourselves and someone else. Whenever we look for truth-with-a-capital-T, we're likely to find only shades of gray-with-a-lower-case-g. Each person brings his or her unique perspective to every interaction.

Many people respond to this lack of clarity by rejecting their feelings about an interaction with another person. If the truth of the matter isn't clear, that means their feelings might be wrong, so it's best to discard them and start over. Wipe the slate clean.

But, as we've seen, once feelings are set in motion, there's no getting rid of them.

In the last chapter, Tony, the new home-owner who regretted how his first conversation went with his next-door neighbor, found himself thinking, "I shouldn't be so upset about this." In making that statement, he immediately assumed his feelings were wrong.

Tony's reaction is as understandable as it is common-place.

As children we learn in many different ways that if we're having unpleasant feelings, we're wrong *and* it's our own fault. Through repeated training, formal and informal, we become convinced that, when we experience unpleasant feelings, we're either stupid, mistaken, or both.

We get that impression from instructions like these:

"You shouldn't feel that way. She's doing the best she can."

"That's no reason to get mad about it."

"Stop crying—it's no big deal."

"You should be glad it's not worse."

These well-intentioned words of popular wisdom are passed from generation to generation, stunting our emotional growth. They shut down our natural responses to the world around us, stick in our minds and become automated messages that we re-send to ourselves regularly: "I shouldn't feel that way; she's doing the best she can," etc.

No wonder we constantly second-guess our own emotions! We learned early and well that, whatever we might feel about something, especially if it's bad, we're probably wrong.

But let's review. Can we be wrong about what another person said or did? Of course we can. But can we be wrong about *how we feel*? Not if we're honest with ourselves.

It's never too late to undo the training that taught us to question our own experience. Now that we're adults and we know how to play well with others, it's safe to reclaim our emotional integrity.

We can choose to accept that what we feel is valid and to advocate for ourselves, if necessary.

There's another aspect to this worry. The concern that our feelings might be wrong can sometimes function as a defense against healthy conflict. If I'm not sure I'm right to feel the way I do, then I can convince myself I shouldn't talk about my feelings to the person who hurt me. Because maybe he didn't mean it.

It's easier for me to convince myself he didn't mean it than it is for me to be honest with him about the fact that he hurt me, even when doing so would improve our relationship by creating more intimacy.

Be alert to using "My feelings might be wrong" as a way to avoid a constructive confrontation.

I mentioned in Part I that you can't choose your emotions. Once your feelings are activated, whether you think you're right or wrong, it's pointless to try not to have them. It's like trying to put a baby back once it's been born—any attempt to do so is very ill-advised.

Your only efficient choice is to embrace your feelings, whatever they are, and get on your own side. If you're wrong about any part of it, you can say you're sorry later for your behavior. But you need never apologize for your emotions.

For all intents and purposes, your feelings are never wrong.

Worry #2: I don't want to be negative

Well, of course you don't. No one likes to be that negative person who brings everyone down. Rachel didn't want to be "negative" about the vacation she failed to enjoy with her friends, and her worry is shared by many Americans. We hate negativity. Or, to put a more positive spin on it, we love to be positive!

I recently did an Internet search for the phrase "how to be more positive" and got more than TWO *BILLION* results. It's clear that being positive is something people really want. But why? Leaving aside the stereotype of the negative person for a moment, there are two main reasons we love positivity so much.

First, adopting a positive attitude makes it easier to be productive. Try doing a good job at anything when you're feeling mopey. It doesn't work and it's no fun trying. Americans worship productivity almost as much as we adore being positive, so it feels almost immoral to let "negative" emotions take away the energy we need to work cheerfully and hard. If productivity is our engine, positivity is the fuel that makes it go.

But, even apart from the productivity cause, being positive is desirable in itself because it feels so good. It may be even more addictive than caffeine, nicotine, or video games. We want to be positive mainly so we can avoid feeling bad.

Which brings us to the second, more obvious, reason we love positivity: Those negative feelings *hurt*. It stinks to be sad, lonely, jealous, defensive, etc. Since we're more productive and more comfortable without negative feelings, we counsel ourselves and each other, "Don't be so negative." (That strikes me as a pretty negative thing to say, by the way. I'm just saying.)

We actively cultivate positivity through repeating affirmations, journaling about gratitude, and suppressing thoughts of hardship, hazard, or inequity. We act as if there's only one side to the experience of being human, when in fact there are two.

We lose something by not allowing ourselves to dwell on the negative sometimes, whole-heartedly.

We need to dwell exactly where we live and thrive, which is in touch with our authentic selves—the part of us that feels. Refusing to embrace emotions we consider negative means rejecting ourselves. If you think about it, refusing to be negative *is* negative: We're negating or denying our own experience.

If you want to be more genuinely positive, culti-vate self-compassion, self-acceptance, and tolerance for every emotion that arises within you. You'll find your-self developing a naturally positive outlook that runs deeper than before.

If you're serious about not being negative, don't negate your own feelings.

Worry #3: It's no use dwelling on the past

Having feelings about something that's already happened, and can't be changed, was one of Rachel's concerns about (w)allowing in her bad memories from her vacation in Mexico. It's also a strict no-no, according to conventional wisdom. Check these out:

"It's no use crying over spilt milk."

"What's done is done."

"You can't rewrite history."

"The past is dead; let it go."

You can probably think of dozens more tidbits of daily wisdom that pass back and forth between us about the fact that we need to look ahead, not back.

I'm not going to argue about the past being over and done with. Unquestionably, what happened in the past happened exactly the way it did, and nothing you or I can do will change it. Yet just because something can't be changed doesn't mean we're not allowed to have feelings about it. Right? If you still have an emotional response to something from your past, your emotions are occurring in the present. They're with you here and now, which makes them current. You're not "hanging on" to bad feelings from the past. It's the other way around; your feelings have got hold of *you*. And for good reason.

You were injured in some way back then. Maybe in a lot of little ways you hardly remember, maybe in one or several big ways. You were angry, or sad, or scared, or all three. The proof is in the feelings that are in you now. They're not there because of something you ate or because you insist on feeling bad about the past. Why on earth would you do that to yourself if you had a choice? You wouldn't. You aren't doing it to yourself.

The reason you have feelings about the past today is that you didn't have the room, the time, or the support to fully experience those feelings back then. Instead, you had to tuck that emotion away, along with the vulnerable part of yourself it was attached to, in order to continue with the task of moving forward in life. But the feelings never went away. They couldn't. Remember the Escalation Cycle from Chapter 1? Stuffed feelings are trapped and can't go away until they're fully felt.

Now that wounded part of you, and the pain that's attached to it, is showing up again, hoping to be reintegrated so that you can be whole again. Will you push yourself away saying, "You missed your chance, so get lost"?

In the legal system, there's a statute of limitations on the prosecution of certain crimes; after a certain period, perpetrators can no longer be indicted, charged, or punished. After that point, those who seek justice for those crimes are simply out of luck.

However, there's no such thing as a statute of limitations on feelings. The pain from the past that's making itself known today needs and deserves your attention today. It's a good day for the resolution process whenever old feelings reappear, no matter how many weeks, months, or years have gone by.

Wallowing constructively in feelings that began a long time ago opens the door to a permanent healing of recurring emotional pain. It allows you eventually to tap into reserves of energy and joy you didn't even know you had, and helps you loosen restrictive patterns of relating to others.

If something is bothering you right now, it's not in the past. It's in the present. So now is the right time to deal with it.

Embrace all your feelings, especially old ones. They're an important part of you.

Worry #4: If I feel it, I have to do something about it

Like many people I know, college student Rachel from Chapter 6 believes that feelings and actions go hand in hand. She was raised to believe that an emotional response is only worth noticing if you're prepared to do something about it. In her case, she assumes she has to talk to her friends about what happened in Mexico.

This confusion between *feeling emotions* and *doing something to resolve them* is common enough that you may never have consciously thought about the distinction before you read Chapter 3.

I once had a session with a new client that reveals the workings of this confusion. Let's call the client Owen.

Owen was a gentle soul who came in to talk about problems he was having with his sister, who was obviously a very important person in his life. According to Owen, this sister was constantly doing and saying things that hurt his feelings. He had multiple accounts of his sister's beastly behavior, which he offered one after another with considerable heat.

But when I asked Owen if he was angry at his sister, he froze and stared at me as if I'd just pulled his brain out of his ear and tried to hand it back to him.

In response to my question, Owen told me that he couldn't possibly confront his sister about her behavior—something I hadn't suggested.

Based on his reaction, Owen's reluctance to admit being angry at his sister (despite exhibiting every anger cue in the book) was likely about not wanting to have to tell his sister he was angry. I assume he knew his sister well enough to guess how such a confrontation would go.

Owen was a widower and had few friends. He valued his sister's companionship no matter how troubled the relationship, so the thought of losing her was too much to bear. So dangerous did it feel to confront this sibling that he couldn't afford to be honest about his feelings even when his sister wasn't present. He was convinced that, if he admitted to being mad at his sister, even to me, he'd have to tell her and, in doing so, lose her forever. What Owen didn't know was that it's possible to feel something, give yourself the compassion you need, and not necessarily take any other action. Eventually Owen did decide to tell his sister something about how her behavior affected him, and, after a few months of painful renegotiation, their relationship improved.

Whether it's a good idea to talk with someone whose behavior upsets you depends on the relationship. The point here is that, in all relationships, telling the other person about any particular feeling is optional. Whatever emotions you have, you're free to have, without doing one darn thing about them.

You must allow yourself this privacy so that you'll be free to explore and embrace all your emotions, even if they're scary. Ironically, once you allow yourself to feel and not share, you may find yourself sharing more, and more productively.

What if you feel like killing someone? Of course you're not going to act on that impulse! Is it still okay to feel angry or even full of hate? It has to be. Whatever emotion is there, it's there. Your only good choice is to allow it to be. Don't allow it to rule your actions, but just let it be there. If you act on your feelings, your behavior will be judged—by you and by others. Your actions might be moral or immoral, reasonable or unreasonable, effective or not. But if you don't act, if you simply feel, there's no question of morality, reasonableness, or effectiveness. So go ahead and feel your feelings. Decide separately what, if anything, to do about them.

Just because you feel something, doesn't mean you need to do anything about it. You're allowed to notice a feeling even if you don't want to act on it.

Worry #5: I'm being self-indulgent

Mark thinks indulging himself in anger and worry over his wife's cancer diagnosis is morally wrong. But is it really self-indulgent to feel miserable? By definition, self-indulgence involves the gratification of a desire. But Mark has no desire at all to feel bad about what's happening. He'd rather not have feelings about his wife's predicament; he'd rather go home and forget all about her surgery, whistling while he cuts the grass as if everything's okay. His real desire is for it all to go away.

But Mark can't have what he desires. He feels all sorts of things about what's happening even though he'd rather not. By acknowledging his emotional response, he's finding the strength (not the weakness) to allow and tolerate that which already *is*.

We would be far better off as a society if all of us could acknowledge and tolerate our uncomfortable feelings in this way. (W)allowing (in) one's true emotions is crucial to society's well-being, because the "allow" in "wallow" provides a social safety valve. Feelings that are bottled up too long can create enough internal pressure to cause a loss of judgment, with terrible results.

Think of the stereotypical stoic male who shows emotion only when he's drunk. When he's sober, his feelings are largely suppressed. He rarely smiles, doesn't talk much; there's not much there to relate to. Or else he smiles all the time, and talks up a storm. But still, he's a self-contained one-man show.

His feelings, good and bad, are locked away, waiting

for alcohol to release them. Once inebriated, the stereo-typical "angry drunk" will become violent, weepy, or both. Alcohol and other drugs melt away emotional inhibition. Whatever's been trapped inside comes out with a vengeance to make up for all that stoicism.

While it may take some time, learning to tolerate his feelings when he's sober through constructive wallowing can help protect him and others from harm. Let's say you're more of an internalizer; you suppress your feelings but you don't lash out at others. You're the only one who gets hurt through being depressed or self-critical or having no energy. If you think you're being self-indulgent by wallowing in your emotions, in addition to looking up "self-indulgent" in the dictionary, I'd like you to consider the following two words: So what?

So what if you *are* indulging yourself? What contract did you sign that denied you the right to any indulgences? Is your only purpose in life to be selfless? Stoic? To take one for the team? Unless you're a bee or an ant, that's a waste of your potential and a poor bet for your quality of life. You know there's more to you than being quiet and sturdy and not having any needs. A coffee table can do that. You're here on this planet to have a human experience. You do have needs. You do have feelings. Indulge yourself. Be human. Stoicism and self-negation have their place in a well-lived life, but when they dominate, you might as well be a piece of furniture.

"Indulging" in feelings is good for all of us, and makes life worth living.

Worry #6: I'm just making myself feel bad

Mark's concern that he's making himself feel bad is the mother of all misconceptions about the (w)allowing process. If you believe you can make yourself feel certain feelings just by turning your attention to them, go ahead right now and make yourself fall in love with someone. (I suggest choosing a person who knows how to cook and owns a set of power tools.) If you can really control how you feel, you might want to put this book down and go write your own about how to do that. It would surely be a bestseller!

In all seriousness, wallowing doesn't mean you're making yourself feel bad, or worse than you already do. It just means you're consciously letting your emotions be exactly what they are, instead of minimizing them or pretending they're not there when they SO are. And isn't that kind of delusion even kookier than making yourself feel bad?

If your feelings seem to grow more painful as you're feeling them, it's only because you're experiencing them head-on instead of at an angle. They're not becoming worse, they're just becoming clearer to you. You're seeing how bad they are—how bad they've been all along, under the surface. If you hang on for the ride, your feelings will peak and then dissipate on their own. If you bail out prematurely and stop the process, you'll have to start again where you left off.

One thing that might make you feel worse during

an attempt at wallowing is thinking about your feelings rather than experiencing them. If you're thinking about what happened in the past or worried about what might happen in the future, you're not (w)allowing in feelings. Rather, your mind is trying to manage them. This might succeed in making you feel worse than you already do, so tread carefully and refer back to the T-R-U-T-H Technique in Chapter 5 for pointers.

Wallowing in painful feelings doesn't create those painful feelings or make them grow worse. All you're doing when you wallow is admitting to yourself that you're in emotional pain, and opening up to the true extent of your emotions.

You can't make yourself feel anything you don't already feel.

Worry #7: I should be grateful it's not worse

This is one of those pronouncements that's so popular I wish I had a nickel for every time I heard it as a therapist. I'm constantly being told by my clients how much worse other people have it than they do. Heaven forbid they should feel sorry for themselves—even though the truth is, they could use the sympathy.

When I invite people to explore their more difficult feelings, they often start by saying, "I don't want to be a baby about it." You'd think being a baby was the worst thing in the world. The International Association for the Advancement of Babies (IAAB) is more than a little annoyed about this, by the way.

I admit I do the same thing my clients do, comparing my own pain to people who have it much worse and minimizing my own suffering. Making comparisons like this may just be something that reasonable people do. We want each other to know that *we understand it could be worse*. Okay, I get that. Let's agree that there are people in the world who have it worse than we do. Agreed? Good. That doesn't change the fact that you're in pain, when you are.

See if you can call to mind the worst physical pain you've ever had. Maybe you get migraines. Maybe it's back pain. A toothache. Whatever it is, picture that you're in terrible pain, and someone comes along and says, "That guy over there just got run over by a truck. You should be grateful you're not him!" As you writhe in your own pain, how grateful do you feel? It's not normal to experience gratitude about anything when you're in pain.

There's always someone unhappier, unluckier, or just plain worse off than you. What does that have to do with your pain? Does it make it hurt less? No.

Pain is pain. Don't make light of yours.

Worry #8: My feelings are draining and/or toxic

This is the concern that drove Natasha to use positive thinking as a shield against her real feelings in the first place. When she was hit by a drunk driver, she decided she needed to make the best of her new situation. That's a noble (not to mention a practical) thing to do, and a good plan on the face of it, but Natasha had feelings that needed her attention *before* she went on to make the best of a bad deal.

It wasn't Natasha's anger at the driver who hit her that was so draining. It was the struggle *not* to feel the anger. And it was her belief that a good person makes the best of things, instead of "indulging" in anger, that made poor Natasha feel so toxic.

Fighting feelings takes huge amounts of mental force. It's draining. But allowing feelings to be exactly what they are takes no energy at all, and can release tension in the mind and body. Exhaustion that occurs after wallowing constructively in feelings is due to a release of built-up tension, assuming you really let your feelings flow, like a baby does (You're welcome, IAAB).

As for anger itself being toxic, there's no such thing as a toxic emotion, period. Struggling against the feelings you have can cause enough stress on your mind and body to make you sick, however. Even joy could become toxic if you fought it long enough. No one's volunteered to do that experiment yet.

It's suppressing emotions—not having them—that's draining and toxic.

Allowing yourself to experience all your feelings releases tension and is good for you.

Worry #9: I don't want to feel this way for the rest of my life

This is the other reason Natasha kept the door closed on her anger for so long; she thought if she let herself feel it fully, she'd be angry for the rest of her life. No wonder she was reluctant to allow herself that feeling. Emotions, as we saw in Chapter 3, are like flowers. They're designed to wither and die once they've bloomed. It takes less than two minutes, according to some recent research, for a particular feeling to move through you. No feeling is constant, and no feeling lasts forever...unless it's never released through wallowing.

Try the following exercise and see for yourself. It takes courage, but the payoff is enormous:

When you're feeling bad, try to feel as bad as you can, for as long as you can. See how long you can hold on to that bad feeling. If you start to feel better, concentrate on trying to feel bad again. You'll understand by doing this that the more you cling to your bad feelings, the more surely they'll leave. What a happy paradox!

Wallowing in your feelings will make it harder for them to stick to you.

Worry #10: I should try to forgive, not hold on to my anger

Natasha's not the only one who believes that she needs to forgive in order to heal. Forgiveness, we're told, is not for the other person, but for ourselves.

Forgiveness is a wonderful feeling, and the idea that you're doing it for yourself is a wise attitude. Unfortunately, like other emotions, foregiveness isn't something you can experience at will. Certainly you can adopt a *policy* of forgiveness. For example, you can decide against suing someone who hurt you. But that's different from experiencing the emotion of forgiveness.

Forgiveness is what's left over when all the bad feelings about what happened have moved through you. It's not necessary—or possible—to make yourself feel forgiveness toward someone who hurt you. It happens naturally, as long as Nature is allowed to unfold in its own way. Forgiveness doesn't lead to healing. It's the other way around. Healing makes way for forgiveness. Don't put the cart before the horse. The only path to forgiveness is through the healing crisis of emotional pain. As long as you haven't fully experienced all the pain, forgiveness is blocked.

And, by the way, forgiveness is made much easier in the presence of remorse. If the person or people who hurt you show no remorse, it's as if they're continuing to hurt you even now. Forcing forgiveness only makes you feel like a bad person when you aren't able to do it, so for heaven's sake, don't even try it. Try forgiving *yourself* for not being able to send loving kindness to those who hurt you. Don't hurt yourself further by assuming you should feel a certain way by a certain time.

Feel your pain, and trust forgiveness to take care of itself.

Worry #11: I don't want to cry

Concerns about crying are prevalent in our culture. Many of us learned when we were young that crying was selfish, petty, childish, irritating, inappropriate, unwelcome, ignored, ridiculous, a nuisance, anger-provoking, or just mysteriously somehow a very bad thing to do.

First, take yourself off the hook; you're not all messed up just because crying isn't your favorite thing. Understand where your aversion comes from, and accept that you feel the way you do about it. You're allowed your preferences when it comes to everything, including crying.

Second, consider other attitudes toward crying. For instance, imagine tears as evidence that something frozen inside of you is thawing. Think of your tears as signs that the cold, hard walls that kept you separated from yourself and others are melting with the warmth of your newfound self-compassion. Isn't that a relief? Or do as my friend's therapist recommended to him, and assume that tears are nothing more than an overflow of emotion. Keep it simple. You can also remember that toxins are thought to be discarded through tears, and other chemicals are released into your system to soothe you from the inside out when you cry. Weeping is Nature's built-in feel-better mechanism.

Third, you don't have to prove anything to anyone by crying when you wallow. If you cry, you cry. If you don't, you don't. Hold it loosely.

Be gentle with yourself about crying. Whatever happens when you wallow, remember to ALLOW.

Worry #12: What if I can't stop the feelings once they start?

It's true: You can't stop feelings in their tracks once they get started. But you don't have to worry that they'll continue forever, or even for a very long time.

I remember a fateful appointment with an endodontist who performed what used to be called a root canal on one of my molars. Suddenly, something he was doing *hurt*. A lot! But when I tried to tell him, he curtly informed me that I couldn't possibly be feeling any pain, and implied that I was being a drama queen (Moi?). He continued to work on the tooth, essentially torturing me until he was done. His reaction to my pain stirred up intense feelings of helplessness in me, and brought on a stream of tears which I was powerless to control.

I was working as an administrative assistant at the time and this happened in the middle of a work day, so I had to go back to the office afterwards. As much as I wanted to, I couldn't stop the tears that were pushing their way out of me. So I did what women have been doing since the Stone Age: I cried in a bathroom stall until I could gather my composure.

(According to scholars, bathroom stalls in the Stone Age were thicker and studier than they are nowadays, completely shielding the occupant from prying eyes and ears. This is doubtless how the tradition got started.)

A feeling might be pushy when it comes, but no feeling lasts forever. Even the most intense ones come in waves. At the very least, you'll get breaks. It took about fifteen minutes for me to completely stop crying that day. Once the last wave was done, it was over. The feelings were intense, but they left me alone once they'd had their way with me.

You don't have to worry about stopping your feelings if you decide to wallow in them. Just make sure to give yourself plenty of time when you sit down to do it. And if feelings catch you off-guard like they did me that day, do what you already know how to do: manage them as best you can till you can get to a "wallowing station."

Feelings can be persistent, but all feelings eventually come to an end. Trust the process.

Now that I've addressed a dozen of the most common concerns, I hope you'll feel encouraged to put aside some time to make constructive wallowing an integral part of your life. Use the T-R-U-T-H Technique or come up with your own self-compassionate way to (w)allow in your emotions.

In the next chapter I'll give you a set of tools that

will build on your progress and pave the way for even more personal growth. You'll find a unique collection of exercises that will help you better understand and appreciate yourself, be more comfortable with all your emotions, and connect to a fuller, more passionate life.

Summary

- For all intents and purposes, your feelings are never wrong.
- If you're serious about not being negative, don't negate your own feelings.
- Embrace all your feelings, especially old ones. They're an important part of you.
- Just because you feel something doesn't mean you need to do anything about it.
- Indulging in feeling is good for all of us and makes life worth living.
- You can't make yourself feel anything you don't already feel.
- Pain is pain. Don't make light of yours.
- Suppressing emotions is far more toxic than having them
- Wallowing in your feelings will make it harder for them to stick to you.
- Feel your pain, and trust forgiveness to take care of itself.
- Be gentle with yourself about crying. Whatever happens when you wallow, remember to ALLOW.
- Feelings can be persistent, but all feelings eventually come to an end. Trust the process.

Chapter 8

Your Wallowing Workout: Ten Activities for Heart and Mind

This chapter offers exercises that will support you in using the T-R-U-T-H Technique outlined in Chapter 5 and will help you become more comfortable with emotions generally. You can use these activities either as a warm-up before trying the Technique, or as a way to deepen your wallowing practice and strengthen your "feeling muscles." Think of them as emotional calisthenics, or as fun things to do in your spare time— whatever works for you.

It's not possible to arrange the activities so that the easiest ones come first, because everyone's different; what's hard for me might be easy for you, and vice versa. So it's best to read through all of them before selecting an exercise that's easy enough not to be too daunting, but challenging enough to stretch you a little.

Start with the easier activities and work toward ones that are harder for you; you need to be able to touch your knees before you can touch your toes. Some of these might seem almost too easy. But if you try them out, I think you'll find that each activity is easier to read about than it is to actually do. I'd like you to gently expand your comfort zone. So go easy, but go.

Nature or Nurture?

Every one of us is, to a certain degree, a product of our upbringing. The purpose of taking a feelings history is to understand how your past affects your approach to emotions today. You can be certain that it does.

Although the temperament you were born with does appear to play a role in your emotional reactions to life, you didn't come into this world with maladaptive emotional responses programmed into you. If it feels scary to be close to people, there's a reason, or more likely multiple reasons, to be found in your history. You may have come from the factory with a shy disposition, but fearing emotional intimacy in relationships is *not* something you were born with.

Similarly, having a fiery disposition may be in your genes, but it doesn't make you lash out at people or throw things. How you *handle* your emotions is learned by observation and/or conditioning, regardless of temperament. This is why some fiery people are cops and some are criminals.

So take a look back at where you've come from and consider what you might have picked up since you were born. Keep in mind that the earlier you learned something, the less likely you are to be aware that you learned it from someone else and the more likely you are to believe it's just the way you are. This could be an eye-opener.

If possible, write your answers to the questions below in a journal to give yourself more space to explore them. For your convenience, Table 2 is reprinted in this chapter to remind you of some feeling words. It's on page 188.

Activity 1: Feelings History

Which emotions were allowed in your family? Who was allowed to have them? _____

_____

_____

_____

How did people in your family deal with emotions?

_____

_____

_____

Who taught you the most about what to do with your feelings? _____

_____

_____

_____

Was there a song or a story you loved when you were young? How did you feel when you heard or read it? __

_____

_____

_____

What is your earliest happy memory?_____

_____

_____

_____

What is your earliest painful memory?_____

_____

_____

_____

What feelings do you remember from your first romance?_____

_____

_____

_____

Describe a time in your life when you felt...
Proud_____

_____

Peaceful _____

_____

Overjoyed _____

_____

Sad _____

_____

Angry _____

_____

Scared _____

_____

Other_____

_____

Choose some feeling words to describe each decade in
your life, e.g., "teens—angry, scared; twenties—hopeful,
happy, etc." _____

_____

_____

_____

What are some feelings you've experienced often in the
past year? _____

_____

_____

_____

What about the past month? _____

_____

_____

_____

The past week? _____

_____

_____

_____

Table 2. Some Feeling Words

Painful	<···>		Pleasant
Afraid	Inadequate	Accepted	Optimistic
Angry	Inferior	Amused	Peaceful
Anxious	Insecure	Appreciated	Pensive
Apathetic	Insignificant	Appreciative	Playful
Ashamed	Irritated	Aware	Pleased
Betrayed	Isolated	Calm	Powerful
Bewildered	Jealous	Cheerful	Present
Bored	Lonely	Cherished	Proud
Confused	Lost	Close	Respected
Defensive	Nervous	Confident	Respectful
Depressed	Off-balance	Connected	Sensuous
Despondent	Overwhelmed	Content	Stimulated
Disconnected	Regretful	Creative	Successful
Discouraged	Rejected	Daring	Surprised
Envious	Ridiculous	Elated	Thrilled
Embarrassed	Sad	Energetic	Trusting
Empty	Stuck	Engaged	Valuable
Frustrated	Stupid	Excited	Whole
Furious	Trapped	Fascinated	Worthwhile
Grieving	Unacceptable	Free	
Hateful	Unlovable	Grateful	
Helpless	Unsuccessful	Grounded	
Hopeless	Unwanted	Hopeful	
Hostile	Unworthy	Important	
Hurt	Wary	Included	
		Joyful	
		Loving	
		Nurtured	

Self-Compassion

The next two activities will be difficult if you don't have much experience being kind to yourself. If you feel like a ninnyhammer while working on self-compassion, ask yourself, "Why do I feel like a ninnyhammer? And what *is* a ninnyhammer, anyway?" It's a very foolish person, but the question is: What is it about being kind and loving to yourself that makes you feel that way? Why do so many of us feel foolish and even phony when we try to be kind to ourselves?

We'll return to that all-too-common issue in Chapter 9. Just be aware of that part of you that thinks it's wrong, fake, or foolish to show yourself some love. It's not really a part of you, it's just a relic from an earlier time in your life, masquerading as you. It's a defense mechanism designed to keep you in line and therefore, in a weird way, safe. Consider whether you still need that mechanism, or whether you can discard it now in favor of the safe, enfolding arms of self-compassion.

Activity 2: Practice Loving Yourself
You can do this while riding an elevator, waiting in line, or running a bath. Anytime you find yourself with even one minute on your hands, you can put away that addictive electronic device and take the opportunity to cultivate a loving relationship with yourself.

Completing this exercise daily will help you establish a friendlier tone in your self-talk, which will help you move mountains in your life. You'll get better with practice, so keep it up. Here we go...

Before you begin, relax any tense areas in your body and breathe normally.

Start by noticing your feet. There they are, at the ends of your legs, doing what feet do. How do they feel?

Send them your love.

Silently say something loving to them, like "I love you, feet." Or, "Hey, thanks for all your hard work today." If that feels like too much, try toning it down: "You're not so bad, feet."

Picture your feet being pleased to hear that from you.

Imagine exchanging a secret smile with your feet.

Next, move up to your calves. Send them some love. Silently say something loving to them. It doesn't have to be sophisticated, deep, or elaborate. "You are nice and curvy, calves" is perfectly fine. Just make sure to choose a message you can believe in, and mean what you say.

Imagine that your calves appreciate your message, and that they smile back at you before you say goodbye and move on...

...to your knees. Send them love, too.

Silently say something nice to your knees, just as you did for your feet and your calves. Imagine that your knees hear and appreciate what you say to them. Exchange a feeling of goodwill before moving on.

Take your time and move all the way up your body, saying kind and loving things to each part or area. Don't forget your heart, lungs, stomach, and any other internal organs you feel like loving today.

Remember, your message of love doesn't have to be complicated. It can be as simple as, "You're a good neck."

Concentrate on what it feels like to mean what you

say. If you can't think of anything loving to say, just send love, and imagine your body receiving that love and sending it back to you.

You can do different portions of your body at different times of the day if you don't have time to do the whole thing at once. Just remember where you left off and pick up from there. Or just send your entire body a quick hello and a silent hug. Have your body receive the message and smile back at you.

Activity 3: Letter of Forgiveness to Yourself

Think of a situation you're hard on yourself about.

Write a letter to yourself, starting with "Dear [your name]." Tell yourself you forgive you for what you said/did, and let you know that you understand why it happened that way.

Be a stubborn advocate for yourself, not a critic.

Here's an example:

Dear Jill,

I know you're mad at yourself for letting Jack fall down the hill with that pail of water last summer. I'm writing because I want you to know that I forgive you for not being able to save him when he fell.

You had no idea when you got out of bed that morning that this wouldn't be just another trip up the hill. You'd done that a hundred times without incident. There was no reason you should have been on the lookout for danger.

Jack was always clowning around. When he cried out, "Jill! I'm falling!" it was typical of the kind of prank he used to play on you. How were you supposed to know he wasn't just acting like that boy over in the next town who keeps crying "Wolf!"?

You need to know that I don't blame you for what happened. You loved Jack and it's a terrible loss for you. You deserve to mourn that loss without holding yourself accountable for it.

I have only sympathy for you. That tumble you and Jack took had a terrible impact on your life; I hope you won't let it define who you are.

With love,
Jill

If it helps you to imagine you're writing the letter to someone else, do it. It will be addressed to you, and you're going to read it when you're done. If it helps you take in the compassion by imagining the letter coming from someone else, do it.

Just be sure to sign off with love when you're finished writing, and to open yourself up to the love while you read.

Notice self-critical thoughts popping up as you write the letter or as you read it. That's okay; they were there yesterday, they're bound to still be here today.

It will take time to make the shift toward a consistent tone of self-compassion. Register those self-critical thoughts if they're there, and do the activity to the best of your ability.

Activity 4: Letter of Apology to Yourself

If you've been steeped in self-criticism for years, it's time to tell yourself you're sorry. A new day is dawning, one in which you discipline yourself with love, not with fear.

If it fits for you, start with something like this:

Dear _____,

I'm writing to let you know how sorry I am that I've been so hard on you. I thought being critical would help keep you on track. I was worried that, if I let up, you wouldn't grow or achieve anything. I was wrong.

I realize now that I made you feel terrible. Instead of helping you grow, I made you shrink. Instead of empowering you, I robbed you of your power.

Next, apologize to yourself for specific things. Only write down things you can actually feel at least a little bit sorry about. Don't write it if you don't mean it. You may have to leave some apologies for later.

For each transgression, demonstrate your good intentions by indicating that you understand what you did, and why it was hurtful. Below is a sample.

I regret calling you fat this morning when you stood on the scale. You didn't need to hear that from me. The more I yell at you, the more you eat. I'm so sorry for the pain I've caused you about your body.

I was wrong to go after you for forgetting to ask the doctor about medication during your appointment yesterday. She was obviously rushed, and you did remember to ask all your other questions. You did very well in the circumstances.

While I'm at it, I'm also sorry I said your spinach pie wasn't any good. Everybody said it was delicious, and Elijah, who never eats anything, had two helpings. I was trying to keep you on your toes by doubting your abilities, but I see now that it was misguided and unnecessary.

When you've apologized for the things you regret, sign off with a conclusion and a heartfelt wish for a better relationship in the future. You can use the following, or make up your own conclusion and sign off.

In short, I'm sorry for having been mean to you. I will do better in the future, starting right now.

With deepest regret and lots of love,

_____

You may be tempted to send loving thoughts or write kind letters to others instead of yourself. Resist that temptation for now; it's only there because it's easier to send compassion away than to take it in.

Don't be too concerned if it feels a little bit kooky to write these letters, or if you don't feel much when you read them. That's par for the course; you'll feel insincere as long as you're identifying with the critical, unforgiving voice. Don't give up. It will take time and effort to change your relationship with yourself, but it's worth it. Once you've written one letter, consider it the beginning of a letter-writing campaign that will happen over time.

Enlist the help of a good friend if you need it to edit your letters, making sure they're packed with compassion and free of shaming or blaming language. Then go ahead and mail them to yourself. Receiving a letter in the mail will make it feel more like a real letter.

The first loving letter you write to yourself is a solid step toward writing yourself letters of forgiveness and apology that are more and more heartfelt. Eventually, your efforts to be kind to yourself will make a dent in your self-critical stance, and you'll enjoy the company of an inner friend instead of an inner critic.

Getting in Touch with Feelings

Some people report feeling overwhelmed, anxious, or downright frightened when strong emotions come up. If this sounds like you, then you should know that it's impossible to feel anxious in a relaxed body.

To avoid undue emotional anxiety, you must know how to physically relax.

Two of the best known relaxation techniques are diaphragmatic or belly breathing, and progressive muscle relaxation. I'll go over the basics of them here, but I encourage you to read more widely if relaxation is difficult for you, or if you suffer from anxiety. There are millions of words available in print and on the Internet about how to relax using these and other techniques. This is just a crash course to get you started.

Activity 5: Relaxation

For both exercises, get comfortable in a seated or lying-down position and remove constricting items of clothing. If you're sitting, make sure your feet are flat on the floor and your back is either straight or resting against something.

Belly Breathing Put one hand on your chest as if saying the Pledge of Allegiance and the other on your stomach as if to say, "I can't believe I ate the whole thing." Breathe normally, through your nose if possible. Notice which hand—the one on your chest or the one on your stomach—moves as you inhale.

The goal is to breathe into the lower parts of your lungs, not just into your chest. Try to send the breath down, down, down into your abdomen as you inhale, while letting your stomach expand. The hand resting on your chest should become less mobile than your stomach hand, which should move in and out noticeably with every breath.

Deep breathing like this is inherently calming. Practice it when you don't need to; as with a fire drill, you don't want to wait till there's an emergency to try it out.

You can use belly breathing whenever you want to feel more calm and centered. It will help you anchor yourself in your body, and in the present moment.

Progressive Muscle Relaxation The purpose of progressive muscle relaxation is to train yourself to notice tension in your body and to learn how to consciously relax the areas of your body where tension creeps in.

Start at one or the other end of your body, let's say your head. Keeping the rest of your body as relaxed as you can, gently tense the muscles in your forehead for a few moments. If it's hard to isolate those muscles, picture a pencil lying on a flat surface and imagine trying to pick it up using only your forehead.

Let go of the tension and let your forehead relax more and more until it's so relaxed it feels like your eyebrows might slide right off. Take at least as much time with relaxing your forehead as you took making it tense. Experience the relaxation; note how different it feels from when it was tense.

Repeat this procedure with your jaw, neck, shoulders, arms, hands, torso, buttocks, thighs, calves, and feet. You might want to customize this exercise if you know of particular areas where you carry tension.

For some strange reason, I often find myself clenching my triceps, the muscles in the back of my upper arms. You might hold tension in your scalp, neck, back, feet, or anywhere in between.

You might be able to find free interactive media on the Internet to help you relax, but if not, relaxation-training audio recordings are available through your library and/or in stores.

Activity 6: Art Project

Think about a situation that triggers strong emotions in you, and create an image that represents your feelings. You can do this activity if you don't have a specific situation; just create an image of whatever feelings you're experiencing.

The image may be as specific or as abstract as you like. It can be flat like a picture or three-dimensional like a sculpture.

Allow the colors and shapes you choose to reflect your emotions. If you like, include words in your image. Maybe give it a title, such as "My Grief" or "How I Feel About XYZ." Concentrate on capturing your *feelings* in your image, not just the facts. You don't have to build a scale model of your office just because you're feeling strongly about something at work.

It's best to make your image with the assumption that no one but you will ever see it. That will ensure you the freedom to follow this activity wherever it may take you. Allow the image, as you create it and when you take a step back and look at it, to take you toward and into whatever it is you're feeling. Know that your emotions are safely contained in the image you create; you don't need to do anything else with them right now.

Avoid focusing on your artistic abilities. Don't manipulate the image to make it more interesting, coherent, or palatable for others. The outcome doesn't matter; it's the *process* of creating your image that's valuable. What comes up for you as you create a representation of your feelings?

After you're done, there will be options. You might decide to destroy your image, or to keep it as a reminder. You might share it with someone close to you, or with the public, or with no one at all.

It may be interesting to store your image somewhere secure and revisit it a month, a year, or ten years from now. You may even decide to create a series of pieces, mapping your emotions about a specific or general subject over time.

Activity 7: Listen to Your Heart

The more you actively listen to your heart, the more your heart will open to you. This will give you an inner guide for your journey through life. Your heart can replace an imaginary drill sergeant as your constant companion.

TRUST YOUR HEART

"As soon as you trust yourself, you will know how to live."

~ JOHANN WOLFGANG VON GOETHE

"Go to thy bosom, knock there and ask your heart what it doth know."

~ WILLIAM SHAKESPEARE

"We have all a better guide in ourselves, if we would attend to it, than any other person can be."

~ JANE AUSTEN

"Nothing is less in our power than the heart, and far from commanding we are forced to obey it."

~ JEAN-JACQUES ROUSSEAU

"The heart of a fool is in his mouth, but the mouth of a wise man is in his heart."

~ BENJAMIN FRANKLIN

"Our heart always transcends us."

~ RAINER MARIA RILKE

"The seat of knowledge is in the head, of wisdom, in the heart."

~ WILLIAM HAZLITT

"Trust yourself. You know more than you think you do."

~ BENJAMIN SPOCK

If you have trouble making decisions, listening to your heart will provide you with valuable information that might have been missing before. Without knowing your real feelings about something, you can't make good decisions, especially about an important career move or relationship.

How to Connect with Your Heart

When you have some time and privacy, get comfortable and place a hand over your heart.

Breathe normally for a minute. Then...

Imagine that each breath you take is nourishing your heart.

As you inhale, each breath feeds, soothes, and nurtures your aching heart. Imagine your heart being grateful for your breath. When you take a breath, your heart is nourished.

Breathe into your heart.

It may be that just the intention of breathing in nourishment for your heart will elicit a wave of emotion. That is your heart speaking to you. Stop there and just listen.

Be with your feelings and know that, in this moment, you're hearing from a part of yourself that is normally hesitant to speak.

As painful as it may be to make contact with your wounded parts through connecting to your heart, it's also something to celebrate. In this moment of witnessing your own pain, you are becoming whole again.

If simply breathing into your heart doesn't bring you into direct contact with feelings, you may need to ask just the right question.

Ask your heart whatever question comes to mind. You'll know your heart is speaking to you if you start to feel emotions.

You might ask your heart:

"What do you need?"

"What are you feeling?"

"What do you want me to know?"

Or you might just raise a topic:

"My career"

"Jim's estrangement from the family"

"Dad's health"

...and see what's in your heart about it.

When I do this exercise, I don't use words. I use my breathing to send my heart a non-verbal intention whose message is, "I'm listening."

Some days, my heart doesn't seem to have much to say. This usually happens when I'm distracted by day-to-day busy-ness or just in a productive, rather than reflective, mode.

If you don't hear from your heart, don't worry. Try again another time. Your willingness to listen is an act of self-acceptance, which is like a megavitamin for your core.

There's a season for every awareness activity, and an awareness activity for every season. If you find an activity in this chapter that doesn't seem to speak to you today, try approaching it again in a little while.

Daily & Weekly Exercises

Activity 8: Know Yourself

Getting to know yourself better through this or any self-knowledge activity is a valuable supplement to all the activities described in this book. It's hard to wallow constructively unless you know who's wallowing, and in what.

The following is a silent game you play in your head as you go about your day. The only rule is this: Whatever you pay attention to, no matter how small or inconsequential, you must decide whether you like it or you don't like it.

Here's what it looks like. You're getting ready for work in the morning and you're eating cereal. You think to yourself, "Do I like this cereal? Or do I not like it?" Don't accept a neutral answer; choose "I like it" or "I don't like it." You can always change your mind next time. Just go with how you feel about the cereal right this minute.

Let's say you take the bus to work in the morning. As you stand there waiting for the bus, noticing the weather, the time of day, etc., ask yourself whether you like or don't like waiting for the bus. Once you've made your decision, move on to the next thing.

Do you like taking the bus to work? Do you like your desk? Your chair? Do you like this or that coworker? Do you like starting the day by returning phone calls? Do you like your lunch? Etc., etc., etc.

Look for things to evaluate in the moment. If something is neutral or you're not sure, force yourself to choose either "I like it" or "I don't like it."

Don't be overly concerned about getting it right, especially at first. Accuracy isn't the point of the exercise. Your answers will become more accurate with time and practice.

The point of this activity is to check in with yourself regularly and pay attention to your preferences.

You might find it very hard in the beginning to know whether you like something. You might be tempted to give yourself a neutral answer like "It's okay," "Not too bad," etc. Don't give in. Decide "I like it" or "I don't like it" until you get used to making these decisions.

Knowing how you feel about little day-to-day things makes it easier to know how you feel about bigger things. This particular activity also gives you permission both to have a preference and to change your mind later.

Through this simple game, you'll gather information about yourself that you might not have uncovered if you hadn't bothered to check in.

Now... Do you like this activity? Or do you not like it?

Activity 9: Talk About Feelings

There has been much research on how language affects how we think about things. In short, there seems to be a strong relationship between how we speak and the way we see the world.

According to Dr. Lera Boroditsky[3], an associate professor of cognitive science at Stanford University, "[I]f you change how people talk, that changes how they think. If people learn another language, they inadvertently also learn a new way of looking at the world."

The more you make feelings a part of your everyday conversation, the more familiar and normal emotions will become, and the more likely you will be to take note of your own feelings as they arise. That just might make it easier for you to pay attention instead of letting a backlog pile up that you'll have to deal with later.

Using words for emotions may even make you more readily aware of exactly what you're feeling when you feel it, which will help you with the second part of the T-R-U-T-H Technique process: "Realize what you're feeling."

It's helpful for this exercise to use a word source, so refer to Table 2 as needed, or another source, if you like. Whatever your vocabulary source, try to use a different feeling word in a sentence at least once a day, every day. Use your feeling words to describe:

What you're feeling ("I feel *confused* right now")

What someone else might be feeling ("Did you feel *betrayed* by him?")

What a character on TV is feeling ("Monica seems *elated*.")

What you would feel if a particular thing happened ("That would make me *furious*.")

Use the feeling words in unexpected places such as business meetings ("The customer seems *cheerful* enough in spite of our late delivery"), garage sales ("I'm getting *frustrated* with having to dig for things"), or the grocery store ("I'm *thrilled* to know your pickled herring doesn't contain corn syrup!").

Activity 10: Weekly Feelings Chart

This activity both quantifies your experience of feelings and creates a structure to remind you to be aware of them. If it seems like you're always feeling the same way, or you're not very emotional, here's your chance to find out if you're right.

Use the Weekly Feelings Chart provided in Table 3 on page 207 to track your feelings morning, afternoon, and evening each day for two weeks. You may be surprised to discover that your emotional experience from day to day and week to week is not what you expected.

How to Use the Chart

Under each day, write a feeling word that describes your experience in the morning, afternoon, and evening. Use the "Notes" section at the bottom of each day's column to describe the situation(s) in which you experienced the feeling(s).

Even if you write "not aware of any emotions," try to make a note about your emotional experience three times a day while doing this activity.

Once you're done, you can look for patterns. Do one or two feelings reliably show up at certain times of the day or week? Are you more likely to experience a particular feeling at work than at home, or vice versa? Is there someone or something that's got you preoccupied in a given week?

Table 3. Weekly Feelings Chart

WEEK ONE	Monday	Tuesday	Wednesday	Thursday	Friday	Saturday	Sunday
Morning							
Afternoon							
Evening							
Notes							

WEEK TWO	Monday	Tuesday	Wednesday	Thursday	Friday	Saturday	Sunday
Morning							
Afternoon							
Evening							
Notes							

The Quiz, Take Two!

There's been much discussion about how to deal with feelings since you took the quiz in Chapter 1. I hope that, in making your way through the discussions, ideas and activities presented so far, something has started to shift for you.

If you didn't take the quiz when it first appeared, you won't have a basis for comparison, but you can still use it now. How many of the statements below do you agree with today?

		Agree	*Disagree*
1.	When bad things happen, I try to look on the bright side.	_____	_____
2.	I'd rather not see my friends when I'm unhappy.	_____	_____
3.	There's no sense in crying over something you can't change.	_____	_____
4.	I hate it when I get emotional over small things.	_____	_____
5.	Dwelling on negative feelings only makes them worse.	_____	_____
6.	I like to lead with my head, not my heart.	_____	_____
7.	Anger is a toxic emotion.	_____	_____
8.	I sometimes find my own feelings ridiculous.	_____	_____
9.	It's not healthy to let yourself dwell on negative feelings.	_____	_____

10. I get annoyed at myself when
    I can't snap out of a funk.   _____ _____

11. When I feel down, I try to think
    about things I'm grateful for._____ _____

12. I shouldn't complain; other
    people have it worse than me._____ _____

13. It's best not to think about
    things that make you upset.   _____ _____

14. I often don't understand
    my feelings.   _____ _____

15. I can be pretty hard
    on myself.   _____ _____

16. I'm not comfortable
    with anger.   _____ _____

17. I'm not comfortable
    with tears.   _____ _____

18. I can be overly sensitive.   _____ _____

19. I feel anxious or depressed
    fairly often.   _____ _____

20. I should be able to control
    my emotions.   _____ _____

TOTALS: _____ _____

Compare your score on this quiz with your original score from Chapter 1. Review the scoring key on page 6.

I hope you've shaved at least a couple of points off your original score already. If so, at the very least you've begun the paradigm shift away from beating yourself up about your feelings, toward compassionate self-acceptance and personal growth.

No matter what your score or how it compares to the first one, you can use the quiz as a tool for greater self-knowledge. Here's what to do:

After completing the quiz above, pick one of the twenty statements that you still agree with. If you don't agree with any of them (yay!), pick one that you might *almost* agree with on a bad day, or pick one your family might agree with.

When you've selected the statement you'd like to work with, write it on a small piece of paper or make a note in your trusty electronic device; as long as you carry it with you everywhere, it doesn't matter where you keep it. You mission is to spend one whole day exploring that statement in as much depth as you can.

Resist the temptation to pick more than one at a time. You can always devote a different day to another item. Here are some ways to explore the statement:

- Look for examples and counterexamples as you go about your day.
- Try to remember how you learned to believe the statement.
- Constructively wallow in the feelings your statement evokes in you.
- Express your feelings about the statement to a good friend, or in a journal.
- Write a story, poem, or song about the statement.
- Act as if the statement were *not* true.

We've come a long way together, you and I. And while we've covered a lot of ground, I understand you may still have questions. In the final chapter, I'll answer the ones I hear most frequently.

Summary

- How we deal with emotions is learned when we're young.
- Don't give up if self-compassion feels phony.
- It's impossible to feel anxious in a relaxed body.
- Self-knowledge is necessary to wallow constructively.
- The words we use affect how we think. Use feeling words as often as possible.

Chapter 9

Wallowing Questions & Answers

1. Is there such a thing as NON-constructive wallowing?

As we touched on in Chapter 3, there are activities that masquerade as wallowing that aren't productive at all. But I would argue that those activities are not really wallowing, they're really just acting out destructively. The acting out might be *self*-destructive, like abusing your body with drugs or alcohol, or *other*-destructive, like getting violent with people, animals, or objects. The stereotypical picture of wallowing involves sitting at home all weekend with a bottle of booze or pills (a self-destructive activity). That's not my idea of wallowing.

The only way to make wallowing in feelings

unproductive is by withholding compassion and understanding while you do it. Just feeling bad, and feeling bad *about* feeling bad, won't afford you the healing benefits of a warm embrace when you need it most.

The constructive thing about wallowing well is that it gets you in touch with the truth. Where did my motivation go? Why do I feel so "blah"? Whom am I angry at? *Why would a good person feel the way I do?* Just asking those questions can get things moving again in a way that non-constructive wallowing can't.

2. What if I can't cry?

You don't have to. Just be with your feelings, whatever they are. No crying required.

3. Should I really wallow in GUILT?

You can't. Guilt is not an emotion. It's an assessment of responsibility. In court, "guilty as charged" means the court believes, beyond a reasonable doubt, that the defendant did what he or she is accused of doing.

Guilt and innocence are facts, not feelings. We *are* guilty or innocent; we don't *feel* guilty or innocent. When we say, "I feel guilty," we're really saying something like, "I believe I did something that someone (probably me) thinks is wrong, and I have feelings about that."

Whenever you feel "guilty," look inside with curiosity and caring, to see what else is there.

An uncomfortable emotion that sometimes underlies or accompanies a feeling of "guilt" is anger. We might be angry at the other person for putting us in a position we don't want to be in. Or we might feel angry at ourselves for the same reason.

But underneath the anger is usually something more like shame. Shame is that rotten feeling of being wrong, bad, or unworthy in our being. It's an awful feeling! It's important to become aware of how shame might be motivating you. Otherwise it will control you.

Sometimes the word "guilt" is used to mean remorse—deep regret over something you've done. The big difference between shame and remorse is that, whereas shame is about you as a person, remorse is about your actions, period. When you feel bad about something you've done, try to focus on your actions, not yourself. We all make mistakes. Is there something you can do to make amends?

Remember that only good people feel bad about doing bad things. If you weren't a good person, you wouldn't care so much.

Instead of saying you feel guilty, try saying you feel remorseful, ashamed, regretful, resentful, or angry. Pay attention to which one of those feels most true, and embrace that feeling.

4. What about anxiety? Should I wallow in that?

No. Anxiety is not an emotion, it's a physiological state that often accompanies fear. Anxiety that's a symptom of a medical condition should be treated medically. Non-medical anxiety is always about something, whether you know it or not. Something's making you tense—literally. You might be reacting to a specific situation like public speaking, and/or to conscious or unconscious beliefs, or to bad memories. Your body is activated, and your sympathetic nervous system is gearing up for some action you'll probably never take, like sprinting away from a confrontation.

An oft-overlooked source of anxiety is the presence of other unwanted feelings. I call this "emotional anxiety." This anxiety is both a result of, and a distraction from, emotions we'd rather not have. The best thing to do when you realize you feel anxious is to gently and carefully breathe into the anxiety, opening your awareness to whatever emotions might be there underneath it. You can effectively wallow in those. Use the tools in Chapter 8, or a compassionate friend or therapist, to help you feel safe and confident as you do that.

5. I believe in The Law of Attraction. How can I wallow in negative feelings without attracting negativity?

The 2006 book entitled *The Secret*[4] brought the Law of Attraction into mainstream consciousness. This law, previously illuminated by the likes of James Allen[5], Emmet Fox[6], Napoleon Hill[7], and many others before and after, states that our thoughts create our experiences. That is, whatever we focus on mentally is what we attract to ourselves.

So, for example, if we think constantly about how poor we are, then according to the Law of Attraction we will draw more poverty to ourselves until we change our minds. Once we develop a sensation of wealth, we can't help but experience wealth in our lives. We'll see it when we believe it, in other words.

The law suggests that our thoughts are intentions, and our intentions are powerful enough to create our experience. This idea is both freeing and terrifying; whatever we think about, good or bad, will come to pass in the physical world, according to this law. With that extraordinary power comes extraordinary responsibility to use that power wisely.

If you're nervous about the Law of Attraction bringing you negative energy, wallowing in "negative" emotions might seem like a death sentence for any chance at happiness. But it's not at all. Remember, feelings are neither positive nor negative. They're just feelings.

If you're still uncomfortable with that notion, there's another reason you won't attract negative energy by allowing yourself to feel your "negative" feelings, and that's because the opposite is true!

A feeling, in itself, is not an intention. Therefore it has no attractive power. Only intentions draw energy to themselves, so here's the good news: The intention you hold when you wallow constructively is your intention to treat yourself with compassion. You are saying "Yes!" to loving and accepting yourself, yucky feelings and all.

So, if you're a firm believer in the Law of Attraction, constructive wallowing should be a permanent fixture in your daily routine. With your intention to give yourself room to feel your true feelings, you'll attract more acceptance and kindness into your life.

So go ahead and wallow with all the love, acceptance and compassion you can muster; you'll be putting the Law of Attraction to excellent use.

6. Will wallowing help me feel better about a situation I can't change?

Life doesn't always serve up warm apple pie and ice cream. Sometimes what we get feels more like poison apples and ice picks. Your feelings respond to cues from the environment, so, if your situation is emotionally challenging, your feelings can't change until the situation does.

This might be a good time to reiterate that you can't

choose your feelings, meaning that it's not your fault if you're unhappy with something in your life. Don't believe the propaganda that says every bad thing you feel is because you're choosing the wrong attitude. You're entitled to your feelings, whatever they are. Wallowing in difficult feelings about an ongoing painful situation won't make the situation less painful, but it's neither necessary nor realistic to be happy all the time.

While wallowing won't change the situation itself, it will help you avoid the following:

- Saying or doing things you regret (i.e., acting out feelings)
- Suffering extra stress from holding your feelings in
- Building up a backlog of unfelt emotions that you'll have to deal with later

Keep in mind that your feelings are not the problem. The situation is the problem. Your feelings are just reminding you that the situation is not a good one. Don't shoot the messenger!

7. What if I always have the same feelings in every relationship I'm in?

A tendency to feel the same old way in new situations comes from a tendency to view every situation as being essentially the same—especially relationships. If I'm used to being rejected and abandoned by people close to me, then on some level I'll expect any new relationship to play out exactly the same way my previous ones did, with me being rejected and abandoned by the other person. In psychology, this expectation is sometimes called a schema.

We all have schemas—fixed ideas and expectations about ourselves, others, and the world, based on what we learned early on. Some schemas are more helpful than others, such as a schema that says, "When I'm in trouble, I'm not necessarily alone; there is usually someone willing and able to help me."

Schemas of abandonment, rejection, or worthlessness, on the other hand, often cause problems for us; every time we turn around, we're in pain or afraid again. Someone important to us gets distracted, and we feel rejected. We have a problem, and we believe we're alone with it. Something goes wrong at work, and we feel worthless again. There are many different painful schema types—lots of ways to get hurt over and over again.

The power of schemas comes from the unacknowledged feelings that underlie and fuel them. Remember that emotions we don't consciously embrace always look for ways to be experienced. The seeds of our schema-related feelings were planted long ago, and the feelings themselves are not wrong. They're just late.

Psychologists Jeffrey Young and Janet Klosko[8] call schemas "lifetraps." They write, "We have found that it is very difficult to change deep pain without first reliving it. We all have some mechanisms for blocking this pain. Unfortunately, by blocking the pain, we cannot get fully in touch with our lifetraps."

(W)allow in the actual feelings—not the thoughts—that underlie painful schemas. Don't get hung up on whether your feelings are "right" about today's situation; you're not making a case in court. Just take the opportunity to catch up on some overdue feeling. If you embrace the underlying feelings, you'll see a clearer image of the actual circumstance, because you'll have separated the situation from your feelings about it. Use the tools presented in this book to help you, remember self-compassion, and go gently.

8. If feelings are never wrong, why do they sometimes change when we get new information?

Your feelings are based on your beliefs about what's true in any given moment. You will always respond emotionally according to your beliefs. Obviously, you might believe something that's not true. But your feelings are exactly right for the beliefs you hold. The fact that, when your beliefs change, so do your feelings, means that your feelings are adjusting themselves to the new information, as they should. Feelings are always a match to what you know to be true.

Before you decide to try to change your beliefs in order to fix how you feel, you should know that your beliefs are based on your experiences; you can't pick a new belief just because it makes you feel better. I wish you could.

The fact is, you believe what you believe. When you're convinced otherwise, your feelings will change. Until then, the feelings will stick with what they know.

9. Why can't I just change my feelings by changing my thoughts?

As I said in answer to the previous question, your feelings are based not on your thoughts, but on your beliefs, which in turn are based on your experience. If you really believe something, your feelings will respond accordingly. But just thinking, without a change in your experience, doesn't cut it.

Go ahead and think the following thought: "I am the greatest ice hockey player who ever lived." How much do you believe that? Can you make yourself believe it if you try?

Now, you may happen to play ice hockey, but truly believing you're the greatest player ever is still likely to be a stretch. Heck, even if you *are* the greatest player ever, you might have a hard time really believing it!

Thoughts are not the same as beliefs.

That's why trying to look at a situation a certain way, like other Thought Police techniques for coping with difficult feelings, doesn't work in the long term. It's the same as ignoring your feelings. The "real you" knows what's up.

Taking a different perspective is a good thing to do for its own sake. Even trying to change your feelings about a situation by consciously choosing your thoughts about it might be a winning strategy in the short term. But as a tool for batting away hard feelings, in the long run it only alienates you further from yourself. And that is SO not-productive.

Why not let your feelings be as they are? They'll change soon enough.

10. Why do some feelings seem to last so long?

If feelings are designed to go away after they've been fully felt, why do we continue to love our children or hate that soul-sucking job? Why don't those feelings eventually wither and die?

The answer is that feelings like those are continually being triggered by experience.

It might seem that feelings can last for days, weeks, months, or years, as illustrated in Figure 3 below.

Figure 3. Perceived feeling duration

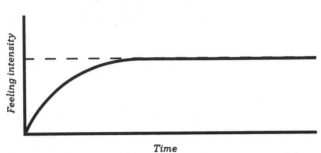

In reality, no feeling lasts for even five minutes. A feeling is always momentary. It might come and go for hours, days, or even weeks or years, but no single emotion lasts more than a minute or two. Remember, even in a garden full of flowers, a single marigold—let's call it Marvin—blooms once, then eventually withers and dies. The garden goes on, but Marvin is no more.

Even though you experience yourself as loving your child, the fact is that there are plenty of times during an ordinary day when your love for your child is not an emotion you're experiencing in the present. It's more of a thought, a protective instinct, or a general policy, not an actual emotion.

When your child does something charming, or looks a certain way, and your heart swells with love, that is a brand-new feeling. It won't last forever, but it will soon be replaced by another experience of the same or a different emotion.

The illusion of emotions lasting for days, weeks, months or years is the result of similar feelings arising regularly enough to create a prolonged emotional tone. This is illustrated in Figure 4.

Figure 4. Actual feeling duration

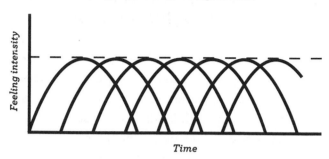

Figure 4 shows that what seems like a fairly constant feeling is actually the same kind of feeling being triggered over and over again.

It's like Marvin dying and being replaced by another marigold, Minnie. Then Minnie dies and is replaced by Mort. And so on and so on. It's a marigold garden, with new members constantly replacing old ones. No matter when you look, there are marigolds.

Every momentary feeling that's allowed to follow Nature's course dies a natural death and never returns.

There's another way feelings can seem to last forever, and that's if they get stuck in the Escalation Cycle. (See Chapter 1.) These are feelings that haven't been able to bloom and are still waiting—usually impatiently—for their turn.

11. How do I cultivate compassion for myself without feeling phony?

I've heard many people say, "When I'm nice to myself, it's like I'm being fake." There's a sense of dishonesty when you start acting differently towards yourself. It's hard to trust that your new kindness is genuine.

This is a real challenge. Being kind and understanding toward yourself in your actions, and even in your self-talk, doesn't necessarily make you feel compassionate toward yourself.

COMPASSION HEALS

"I am not a victim of emotional conflicts. I am human."

~ MARILYN MONROE

"*I* care for myself. The more solitary, the more friendless, the more unsustained I am, the more I will respect myself."

~ CHARLOTTE BRONTË

"Just like children, emotions heal when they are heard and validated."

~ JILL BOLTE TAYLOR

"You yourself, as much as anybody in the entire universe, deserve your love and affection."

~ GAUTAMA BUDDHA

"The most important relationship in your life is the relationship you have with yourself. Because no matter what happens, you will always be with yourself."

~ DIANE VON FURSTENBERG

"No matter what you're feeling, the only way to get a difficult feeling to go away is simply to love yourself for it."

~ CHRISTIANE NORTHRUP, M.D.

"It's not what you say out of your mouth that determines your life, it's what you whisper to yourself that has the most power."

~ ROBERT T. KIYOSAKI

"Compassionate toward yourself, you reconcile all beings in the world."

~ LAO TZU

Based on times when you've been ridiculed, ignored, or rejected by others for expressing uncomfortable feelings, you might believe that it's best to keep a tight rein on your wayward emotions by not indulging them. This, of course, means not indulging yourself...which means skimping on self-compassion.

Your experience tells you that you don't deserve compassion. Otherwise, you would have gotten it far more often than you did from important others. Instead you learned to ridicule, ignore, or reject yourself instead of being empathetic. Your experience also tells you that, if you're not at least a little bit stern with yourself, you'll never get anything done. Or so it seems.

You need new experiences to create different beliefs to experience the feeling of self-compassion.

Kindness and understanding are essential components of compassion. Throughout this book I've told you that you're not responsible for your bad feelings, that you're entitled to feel how you feel, and that you are a good person. You've been exposed to the idea that you deserve kindness, patience, and understanding.

How much compassion have you been taking in as you read? I hope by now that any beliefs you have that don't serve you, about yourself and your emotions, may have shifted just a bit. Small shifts can ultimately accumulate to create big changes. Have you ever had to maneuver your car back and forth a few inches at a time to free yourself from a tight parking space? Unless you're reading this book trapped in your car, I assume you got out eventually. A few inches at a time, this way and that, and then you were on your way down the street.

Set your radar to notice kindness and understanding in others as well as yourself; it may feel more sincere from someone else at first. Use the exercises in Chapter 8 to hone your skill at soaking up that free and essential emotional nutrient, compassion. When receiving good vibes becomes the norm of your experience, your beliefs will shift accordingly.

Once you believe you deserve it, you'll never feel phony being nice to yourself again.

Summary

- The following topics were addressed:
  o NON-constructive wallowing
  o Crying
  o Guilt
  o Anxiety
  o The Law of Attraction
  o Situations that don't change
  o Emotional patterns or schemas
  o If feelings are never wrong, why do they sometimes change?
  o Changing feelings by changing thoughts
  o Feelings that seem to last and last (including diagrams)
  o How to cultivate self-compassion

Chapter 10

How to Choose a Therapist

Y ou've got the knowledge and the tools now to start constructively wallowing on your own. I've shared with you some self-help ideas that have worked both for me and for my clients. But I didn't become a really effective wallower myself without the support of a skilled, feelings-friendly therapist. If you'd like help incorporating this new material into your life, a course of therapy with a counselor or other mental health professional is a great way to go.

If you have a compassionate and non-judgmental friend or relative, in theory they could be every bit as helpful as a professional. The biggest difference is that licensed therapists are bound by a code of ethics to keep what you say confidential, and to put your emotional needs ahead of their own in the relationship.

A good therapist will provide you with a model of how to speak to yourself with kindness, how to pay attention to your feelings and honor them, and how to make sense of your own actions by understanding the emotions that may be driving them.

Your therapist is a person with his or her own relationship to emotions, and every one of us is different. Not all of us received the same training, nor do we do the same things even with the same training under our belts. We're people first, and then counselors, social workers, marriage and family therapists, psychologists, etc. second.

The significance of this is that some therapists are naturally more feelings-friendly than others. Remember that term from Chapter 2? Because feelings-friendly therapists allow themselves to experience and embrace their own emotions, they can be comfortable with your feelings, too. They don't automatically assume that troubling feelings mean trouble.

What Feelings-Friendly Therapy Looks Like

A feelings-friendly therapist will provide a useful example on which you can build your self-talk when you wallow. She or he will do for you exactly what you must do for yourself:

- listen attentively
- reflect what you're saying back to you, so you can see yourself more clearly
- help you make sense of your experiences and emotions
- support you in embracing your own truth, rather than his or her ideas
- honor your emotions by encouraging you to identify and express them

Below is a hypothetical dialogue between a client and a feelings-friendly therapist. Please note that this is just one possibility; no two therapists ever have exactly the same dialogue with a client, no matter how similar their approach to helping.

The client is a thirty-seven-year-old woman who very much wants to be married, but turned down a date six months ago with a new man at work. He turned out to be a very eligible bachelor who started dating one of her friend/colleagues, and now those two are engaged.

The client is struggling with feelings of regret and envy even though she wants to be happy for her friend.

Client: I feel so petty talking about this.

Therapist: Petty? How so?

Client: I'm annoyed that Carly's engaged to Bill! I saw him first. I'm so mad at myself for not grabbing him.

Therapist: You really regret that. What a loss for you. It's so hard to see someone else walk away with what could have been yours.

Client: But I do like Carly. I don't want to envy her. I just want to be happy for her.

Therapist: So you're torn.

Client: Yeah, I really like Carly.

Therapist: And at the same time, she has something you've been wanting for a long time: a partner to start a family with. No wonder you envy her.

Client: And I guess I'm sad.

Therapist: You want so much to start a family.

Client: I really want that, and I could have been starting one now, with Bill.

Therapist: How disappointing, to have missed that opportunity.

Client: What if Bill was my last chance?

Therapist: What a scary thought.

Client: [Crying] It might never happen now.

Therapist: How terribly sad.

Client: Yes. I am so sad right now.

Therapist [with feeling]: I am sorry for your pain.

Client: When I think about Bill, though... He's not exactly my type.

Therapist: What do you mean?

Client: We didn't have chemistry. I don't think I ever would have fallen in love with him. [Describes Bill, noting the things about him that didn't inspire her.]

Therapist: So you might not have wanted to marry him?

Client: No, probably not. Hmm... I guess I'm waiting for the right one. That's why I had no interest in a date. Maybe the right one is really still out there.

Notice that the therapist doesn't judge or try to change the client's feelings, just helps her make sense of them and offers the possibility that conflicting feelings can coexist without canceling each other out. The therapist also doesn't push Carly into a hopeful place; when she's done with her difficult feelings, hope emerges on its own from the remains of her despair.

This feelings-friendly therapist creates a supportive, emotionally safe atmosphere that's perfect for constructive wallowing. As a bonus, the client's esteem for her authentic self will increase and any anxiety that's fueled by hidden emotions will diminish. Everything's out in the open, and it is acceptable.... What a relief!

Where to Find a Therapist

I hear there's a pot of feelings-friendly therapists at the end of every rainbow. But if you don't have the kind of time it could take you to find them, you can locate a therapist by asking people you know, or by looking online at websites where therapists advertise. You can also search the Internet for "counseling," "therapy," or "psychotherapy" in your city or neighborhood. If finances are tight, look for churches and nonprofit organizations that may offer free or low-cost counseling.

Another low-cost option is through colleges and universities that have graduate programs in counseling, social work, or clinical psychology. Students in these programs complete their practical training by seeing clients under supervision. They may work at a center run by the school or somewhere else in the community. You can ask the internship or practicum coordinator of the program for details.

Students may be inexperienced, but they can have outstanding personal qualities that make them exceptional therapists, even compared to more seasoned professionals. The biggest downside of working with a student therapist is that, when the student graduates, your counseling may need to end before you're ready. Ask about a transfer plan before you begin if this is a concern.

I strongly recommend interviewing more than one therapist, especially if you've never had counseling before. By meeting with several people you'll get a sense of just how different we therapists can be from one another.

You'll be able to compare how you feel when you sit down with one therapist as opposed to another. Your feelings are the most important indicator of how well your counseling is likely to go. If you're not quite comfortable with a therapist, trust your instincts. Keep looking until you find someone you feel good about working with.

If you have trouble finding a good therapist, don't

give up. You can get therapy online, so you're not limited by location. In-person therapy is always best, in my opinion; you can read someone better when you're in the same room, and more quickly get a sense of whom you're dealing with. But it's good to know there are other options in a pinch.

Questions to Ask before You Begin

In addition to answering basic questions about his or her training and credentials, your therapist should be perfectly happy to answer any and all of the following questions:

1. "What's your approach to therapy?"

Nowadays, many therapists take what's called an integrative approach, which draws from different theories of how people change. They may say something like, "I tailor my approach to each client."

Customized therapy is terrific, and, in theory, all therapists customize their approach to individual clients. Integrative therapists should have at least one or two formal approaches to therapy that they genuinely believe in, to provide a framework for your work together.

If they specialize in a particular type of therapy, such as Eye Movement Desensitization and Reprocessing (EMDR) or Cognitive-Behavioral Therapy (CBT), ask them to explain it to you. Think about how well their approach fits with your sense of what you need in order to heal.

2. "What's your approach to dealing with negative feelings?"

Watch for language that makes it sound like any feelings should be controlled or eradicated. A feelings-friendly therapist will be curious about your anger, anxiety, or despair. She or he won't be in a hurry to stamp out these feelings, recognizing their value as a tool for self-understanding and growth.

3. "How would you work with me?"

Therapists who know what they're doing will be able to explain what therapy with them will look like...AFTER you give them some information about what's bringing you to therapy, what you've tried before, how well it worked for you, and what expectations or concerns you have about entering therapy.

Even if you've never been in therapy before, you should be able to understand your therapist's answers to your questions. If you ask for clarification and repeatedly don't get it, that could mean that communication between the two of you will be difficult. Trust your intuition and common sense to guide you.

By the way, if the therapist wants to refer you to someone else after hearing your story, don't take it personally! We're not supposed to practice outside the limits of our competence, and so we don't take on clients we don't think we can help based on our training and experience. Take this as a good sign and follow up on the referral.

In addition to the questions to ask a prospective therapist at your first meeting, there are questions you must ask yourself as well. These are the most important questions of all.

Pay attention to how you feel, above all, in the therapist's presence and about his or her dealings with you in general. Reflect on your experience and weigh your answers to the following questions heavily:

Do I feel heard?

Do I feel understood?

Do I feel accepted?

Do I feel respected?

Do I feel safe enough?

If by the end of your first meeting you answer "Yes" to all of the above, your relationship with this therapist is promising.

If you answer "Not sure" to some of them, it may be worth a second meeting, especially if your options are limited.

If the answer to any of these questions feels like a definite "No," keep looking.

Once you find each other, your feelings-friendly therapist will offer you encouragement, support, and compassion as you use the ideas and tools presented in this book to heal your relationship with yourself. Your therapist's gentle attitude toward you will eventually become your own, and you'll carry it with you long after your therapy comes to an end.

Summary

- A feelings-friendly therapist values, and is comfortable with, your emotions.
- A good therapist listens well.
- We sampled a conversation between a feelings-friendly therapist and a client.
- Meet with more than one therapist before choosing one, if you can.
- Ask questions and notice how you feel about the person; trust yourself to know the right fit when you feel it.

YOUR JOURNEY BEGINS

When we met Natasha and Dan at the beginning of the book, both of their lives had changed in a matter of seconds—Natasha when she was hit by a drunk driver and Dan when a bomb exploded, taking his eyesight and part of his hand. The question I asked you then was why, one year later, Dan, who was initially so bitter, seemed to have adjusted so much better than Natasha.

You may remember that Dan raged and cried until his feelings were spent. Eventually, interest and optimism returned on their own. Natasha spent the first year after the accident trying to be positive. To do this, she had to suppress her true feelings about what had happened.

As I hope will now be clear, Dan felt better because he embraced his true feelings. He allowed himself to simply experience what he really felt, as painful as that was. He was able to let his difficult feelings go by letting them run their course.

It was only when Natasha allowed herself to do the same that she began to heal. In time Natasha will find her natural positive outlook again, but this time it will radiate from inside her; it won't be something she's imposing on herself.

For both Natasha and Dan, as well as for you and me, (w)allowing in painful emotions can set us free to be our best selves throughout our lives. But, like most worthwhile and truly healthy activities, it's not a quick-fix solution; it's a lifestyle. Fortunately, now that you've learned to live connected to your feelings, you can't unlearn it. Your shift toward wholeness has already happened if you've worked your way through this book. If you continue to embrace your emotions and your entire self with compassion, you'll have the inner strength and confidence you need to fulfill your destiny.

At this point I expect you've come to better terms with old hurts. You're equipped to deal with all situations that hurt you, understanding that it's the situation, rather than your feeling about it, that's problematic. Your definition of strength may have transformed to include withstanding and expressing painful emotions, rather than denying them.

Like me and everyone else on the planet, you'll continue to be vulnerable to pain and loss; being human, none of us can escape these. But the internal war against those previously frightening feelings is over, and you've won. You can now reclaim all that freed-up energy that used to go into the struggle against yourself, and enjoy your natural resilience and your full capacity for joy.

Instead of worrying about losing control of yourself, you know for a fact that you're always in control as long as you're making a conscious choice to (w)allow in your real feelings.

Your despair has made room in your heart for glee—your anger, for forgiveness. All your emotions have made room for all sorts of other feelings, including motivation, interest, and excitement. There's room in your life now for YOU to emerge from your cocoon and do the things you dream of doing.

This is as far as we go together. I'm honored to have been your guide. Now it's up to you to continue listening to your heart and embracing what you find there. As we part, I want you to hold yourself and all your emotions in high esteem as you take flight and bring your unique gifts to the world. I wish you love, peace, and the fulfillment of your unique purpose.

Afterword

This book was made possible by clients who shared their thoughts and feelings with me in my capacity as their counselor, and also by the thoughtful comments and questions I've received from students in my workshops and classes and readers of my blog (www.tinagilbertson.wordpress.com).

Now that you've read the book, please let me hear from you, too! Let me know what you got from the book, what questions still remain, and what additions would make the book even more useful. You can find me at www.TinaGilbertson.com and on Facebook at www.facebook.com/tinagilbertsoncounselor. My Twitter handle is @TinaGilbertson.

Acknowledgments

The most exciting moment of my life so far was when my then-future literary agent, Janet Rosen, emailed me to say, "I've read your book and I'd like to represent it." I felt as though I'd been handed the keys to a treasure-filled kingdom. And it turned out to be true!

Thanks to Janet's patient stick-to-it-iveness, we found a treasure trove in the form of Brenda Knight and her savvy team at Viva Editions. I'm thrilled to have had their enthusiasm, experience, and energy behind this project.

Many thanks to my intrepid first draft readers: Alison, Gene, Jen, and Jody. I'm glad you guys sent me back to the drawing board. I also owe a debt of gratitude to my second draft readers Alex, Anne, and Lara, and to the lovely group of women who set aside the better part of an evening to provide their thoughtful feedback: Carolyn, Debra, Gayle, Janie, Kimberlee, and Sonila.

A heartfelt thanks as well to Marsha Baker, who gave the third draft an effective once-over with a gentle but exacting eye; and to colleagues Roberta Deppe and Janet Sandell, who provided important feedback on the manuscript as well as enthusiasm for the project.

To my former therapist, Denise Gendreau, and my current mentor, Steve Berman: I'm so lucky you came into my life. To the extent that I'm at all effective as a therapist, I have you both to thank.

To my mom, Iara, for her loving nature, great ideas, and comfort food; my dad, Jerry, who would have been beyond excited about the book's publication; my skeptical brother Charles, who has now officially lost a bet; and Mike Witt noodle, whose belief in me appears to know no bounds, and without whose loving support this book could not have been written... I love you and thank you with all my heart.

Notes

1 Elio Frattaroli, *Healing the Soul in the Age of the Brain: Becoming Conscious in an Unconscious World* (New York: Viking, 2001), 191.

2 David Viscott M.D, *Emotional Resilience: Simple Truths for Dealing with the Unfinished Business of Your Past* (New York: Three Rivers Press, 1996), 77.

3 Lera Boroditsky, "Lost in Translation," *Wall Street Journal,* July 24, 2010.

4 Rhonda Byrne, *The Secret,* 1st ed. (New York: Atria Books/Beyond Words, 2006).

5 James Allen, *As a Man Thinketh,* rev ed. (New York: Tarcher, 2008).

6 Emmet Fox, *Make Your Life Worthwhile* (New York: HarperOne, 1984).

7 Napoleon Hill, *Think and Grow Rich* (New York: Tribeca Books, 2011).

8 Jeffrey E. Young and Janet S. Klosko, *Reinventing Your Life: How to Break Free from Negative Life Patterns and Feel Good Again* (New York: Penguin, 1993), 44.

Bibliography

Allen, James. *As a Man Thinketh*, rev ed. New York: Tarcher, 2008.

Boroditsky, Lera. "Lost in Translation." *Wall Street Journal*, July 24, 2010.

Burkeman, Oliver. *The Antidote: Happiness for People Who Can't Stand Positive Thinking*. London: Faber and Faber, 2012.

Byrne, Rhonda. *The Secret*. 1st ed. New York: Atria Books/Beyond Words, 2006.

Ehrenreich, Barbara. *Bright-Sided: How the Relentless Promotion of Positive Thinking Has Undermined America*. 1st ed. New York: Metropolitan Books, 2009.

Fox, Emmet. *Make Your Life Worthwhile*. New York: HarperOne, 1984.

Frattaroli, Elio. *Healing the Soul in the Age of the Brain: Becoming Conscious in an Unconscious World*. New York: Viking, 2001.

Hill, Napoleon. *Think and Grow Rich*. New York: Tribeca Books, 2011.

Miller, Alice. *The Drama of the Gifted Child*. New York: Basic Books, 2008.

Viscott, David, M.D. *Emotional Resilience: Simple Truths for Dealing with the Unfinished Business of Your Past*. New York: Three Rivers Press, 1996.

Watts, Alan W. *The Wisdom of Insecurity: A Message for an Age of Anxiety.* New York: Vintage, 1968.

Young, Jeffery E. and Janet S. Klosko. *Reinventing Your Life: How to Break Free from Negative Life Patterns and Feel Good Again.* New York: Penguin, 1993.

About the Author

TINA GILBERTSON is a psychotherapist and workshop leader offering individual therapy and classes for personal growth. She and her partner Mike live in Portland, Oregon. *Constructive Wallowing* is Tina's first book.

To learn more about Tina's classes and workshops, and to check out her weekly blog, please visit www.TinaGilbertson.com.

Photograph by Joel Preston Smith.

Index of Terms

Index of Quotations

To Our Readers

Viva Editions publishes books that inform, enlighten, and entertain. We do our best to bring you, the reader, quality books that celebrate life, inspire the mind, revive the spirit, and enhance lives all around. Our authors are practical visionaries: people who offer deep wisdom in a hopeful and helpful manner. Viva was launched with an attitude of growth and we want to spread our joy and offer our support and advice where we can to help you live the Viva way: vivaciously!

We're grateful for all our readers and want to keep bringing you books for inspired living. We invite you to write to us with your comments and suggestions, and what you'd like to see more of. You can also sign up for our online newsletter to learn about new titles, author events, and special offers.

Viva Editions
2246 Sixth St.
Berkeley, CA 94710
www.vivaeditions.com
(800) 780-2279
Follow us on Twitter @vivaeditions
Friend/fan us on Facebook